BETTER DECISIONS

CHRIS GRANT

BETTER DECISIONS

DIRECT YOUR LIFE.
INFLUENCE YOUR WORLD.

WHITE LION
PUBLISHING

Brimming with creative inspiration, how-to projects and useful information to enrich your everyday life, Quarto Knows is a favourite destination for those pursuing their interests and passions. Visit our site and dig deeper with our books into your area of interest: Quarto Creates, Quarto Cooks, Quarto Homes, Quarto Lives, Quarto Drives, Quarto Explores, Quarto Gifts or Quarto Kids.

First published in 2020 by White Lion Publishing
an imprint of The Quarto Group
The Old Brewery, 6 Blundell Street
London N7 9BH
United Kingdom

www.QuartoKnows.com

A catalogue record for this book is available from the British Library.

ISBN 978 1 78131 967 3
Ebook ISBN 978 1 78131 968 0
10 9 8 7 6 5 4 3 2 1
2024 2023 2022 2021 2020

Designed and illustrated by Stuart Tolley of Transmission Design

Printed in China

For Michael Chender
Who taught me about wisdom in action

CONTENTS

INTRODUCTION

'Better decisions' implies better results. If your decision-making improves, you can reasonably expect to achieve outcomes that are closer to what you want. You probably wouldn't have picked up this book if that weren't the case.

It won't surprise you, however, that I can offer no guarantees of success with regard to any particular decision that you might make. Beautifully conceived and executed decision-making processes can produce decisions that turn out to be wrong. That's why decision-making is an art. Yet there is a set of principles and techniques which remain valid across all decisions. That's why decision-making is also a science.

The ideas and techniques contained here aim to help you work more effectively on both sides of this equation. You might be curious to know whether they will be more useful to you at work, or in life more generally. The answer is up to you.

Like anyone, my life has been full of decisions, and in writing this book I have drawn on a broad spectrum of experiences. My work has given me the opportunity to observe, assist and lead somewhere in the region of 2,000 learning groups and leadership teams. Along the way, I've noticed some patterns in how the more effective ones go about their decision-making. I've also had plenty of opportunities to reflect on the decisions I've made – or witnessed – which didn't work out as intended, and the lessons in this book are informed as much by these as by the successes.

Because decisions are so central to all our lives, there is a rich store of traditional proverbs to draw on, many of which offer contrasting or even contradictory messages. 'You've got to be in it to win it' rings true, but 'Look before you leap' makes a lot of sense as well. Chapter 1 sheds light on when to give more weight to one approach than the other, and invites you to reflect on the way you think about the decisions you make.

Of course, many decisions are trivial, but some will be momentous. They could affect just you, your family, your colleagues or a whole community. You may have months to make them or just seconds. My view is that every decision has the same shape. Chapter 2 describes this shape, and encourages you to split your decision-making into three distinct stages: What? So What? Now What?

We all have a head, a heart and a gut. Faced with a decision, any combination of them could come into play . . . Becoming more conscious of how and when to use each of them might be the key that unlocks your potential to make better decisions.

At the heart of the book, Chapter 3 sets out a number of frameworks and approaches to help you capture and organize the data to underpin your decision. In practising these, you'll be coached to look for clues both around and inside you, and to express your inner fox.

But what about when it's not just you making the decision, or being affected by it? Chapter 4 looks at the advantages and challenges of making decisions alongside others. Along the way, it shows you how to identify and navigate some of the classic obstacles to group effectiveness.

Are you a head person or a heart person?

My answer is: 'You're both.' Of course, you have every right to disagree: how can I know whether you're driven by reason or emotion? You may even say that, for you, neither is as important as a third force: intuition.

We all have a head, a heart and a gut. Faced with a decision, any combination of them could come into play. We may tend to favour one over the others, but they're all available. Becoming more conscious of how and when to use each of them might be the key that unlocks your potential to make better decisions. That's why self-awareness is a thread that runs throughout this whole book, but takes centre stage in Chapter 5.

As I've said, there are no guarantees of success, but one thing you can do to help is to accept the invitation made in Chapter 1: to identify some real-life decisions through which you can try out the ideas and techniques in these 20 lessons. This will make it personal. It will switch the focus away from developing a separate 'body of knowledge', so that the real subject matter becomes YOU.

But that's your decision.

HOW TO USE THIS BOOK

This book is organized into five parts and 20 sections covering the ways in which we can navigate the process of decision-making.

Each section introduces you to an important concept,

and explains how you can apply what you've learned to everyday life.

As you go through the book, TOOLKITS help you keep track of what you've learned so far.

At BUILD+BECOME we believe in building knowledge that helps you navigate your world. So, dip in, take it step-by-step, or digest it all in one go — however you choose to read this book, enjoy and get thinking.

Specially curated FURTHER LEARNING notes give you a nudge in the right direction for those things that most captured your imagination.

DECISION - IS BOTH AN A SCIENCE.

MAKING
ART AND

DECISIONS ABOUT DECISIONS

LESSONS

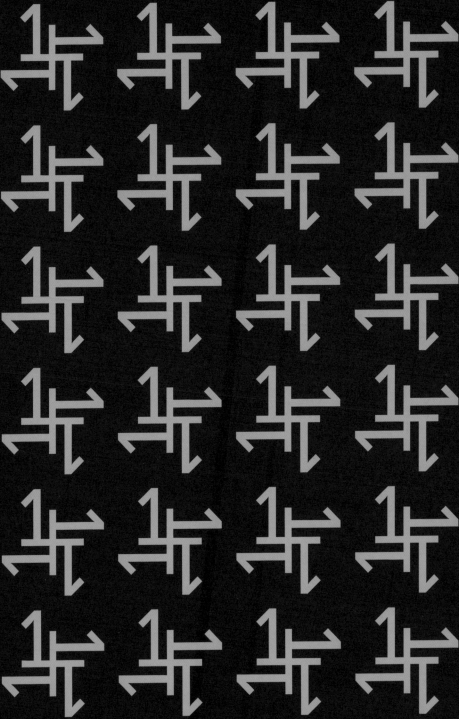

Throughout history, tribes and nations have gone to war to gain or preserve the right to self-determination.

What do human beings need in order to survive and thrive? Obviously, food, shelter and safety top the list. The company of others, a sense of intimacy and belonging are up there too. And not far behind are self-respect and the freedom to choose. Throughout history, tribes and nations have gone to war to gain or preserve the right to self-determination, while in workplaces and hierarchies, status and authority are measured by the decisions that we're allowed to make. As we grow up, we have to wait to cross age thresholds before we can decide certain things on our own behalf.

Our decisions define our lives, but before looking at how to make better ones, we need to define what a decision is, and that's the focus of this chapter.

Perhaps the main reason why some important decisions are never made is that the people who could make them don't believe they have what it takes. In Lesson 1,

we'll consider how to build our decision-making muscles and the confidence to use them. To balance things out before we get too gung-ho, Lesson 2 looks at those situations in which we might decide – at least temporarily – to go with the flow, and not to decide, in order to conserve energy or gain a better view. Lesson 3 invites us to notice that there are different ways to describe a decision, and that choosing one rather than another might provide a short cut, or sometimes lead us down the wrong path. The chapter concludes with a look at the difference between taking a decision and making one in Lesson 4, and enlists the support of sculptors, chefs and one very famous detective to help us build up to our decision, or to narrow in on it.

You're also invited to think about some of the decisions you've made in the past, and others that are in front of you, and we will revisit these decisions throughout the book.

THE RIGHT TO DECIDE

Some say that our decisions make us who we are, and can change the world around us. Others argue that our lives are pre-determined by our genes or upbringing. A third camp points out that decisions made by others constrain us, to the extent that we're really just playing a walk-on part in somebody else's movie.

Guess what? They're all right. Whether we're talking about a whole life, a work project, or how to spend our lunch break, some things are determined for us and some are for us to choose.

Our decisions can transcend the circumstances in which we find ourselves. Sentenced to life imprisonment, Nelson Mandela and his colleagues decided that, to sustain their health and morale, they would take up ballroom dancing. Simply to take and implement such a decision showed that – whatever their circumstances – the prisoners still believed they had the right to determine their own lives, at least to some extent.

In social science, the word used to describe our capacity to make decisions and follow them through is *agency*. The circumstances and factors that limit our capacity to make decisions are referred to as *structure*. Ultimately, the way that we perceive and manage the interplay between these two forces can determine the quality of our lunch hour, our project or our life.

Both agency and structure can be divided into factors generated internally, by ourselves, and externally, by others.

AGENCY

Agency (internally generated)	Structure (internally generated)
E.g. Knowledge	E.g. Insecurity
Agency (externally generated)	**Structure (externally generated)**
E.g. Permission	E.g. Regulations

What's at stake here is not the quality of our decisions, it's whether we're able – or willing – to decide at all. Of course, there will always be factors beyond our control. But we often have more influence than we might recognize.

Max De Pree (1924–2017) ran an office furniture company, and was at the forefront of a movement advocating 'servant leadership'. As the name suggests, a central characteristic of the servant leader is humility. So in his book, *Leadership is an Art,* it comes as a surprise to encounter this bold statement: '*The first responsibility of the leader is to define reality.*'

De Pree's suggestion is that, whether we're talking about leading a team, a family, a community or just ourselves, leadership is all about agency. The leader is a leader because she doesn't just accept circumstances, she shapes them through her decisions.

Whether or not you see yourself as a leader, or have aspirations in that direction, a sense of agency is an essential pre-condition to making better decisions. Believing that you have the right and the ability to decide requires a level of confidence which may come naturally to you, or which may require some work for you to build up.

STRUCTURE

AGENCY AND AFFIRMATIONS

Regularly reminding ourselves that we have agency could be the key to unlocking our decision-making potential, so let's work on our confidence muscles.

If you ask a good fitness trainer how to build muscle, they'll recommend repetitions of targeted exercises. Here, the exercise is to create a positive statement about ourselves as decision-makers, and to write it down or say it enough times for it to lodge in our consciousness. Affirmations, such as 'I can accomplish anything I set my mind to', can promote self-belief and a positive mindset, but they can also invite scepticism, or even a sense of failure and inadequacy.

These negative effects are usually triggered when there is too big a gap between the statement and our actual feelings or perceptions. If you add to this a sense of obligation – that we're only doing this because we've been told to – the whole exercise can feel very false, and actually achieve the opposite of its intended purpose.

To get around the first pitfall, use something that you have actually experienced personally, and find your own words to describe it. To get around the second, let's be clear that this exercise is entirely optional.

01. If you were writing the story of your life so far, and wanted to include a chapter which described a period when you felt relatively 'in control', what would that chapter be called? This title could relate to the issues that you were dealing with at that time, or to the way you felt.

02. List some of the decisions that you made during this period? If only one comes to mind, just write that one down.

03. On your best day, or most positive moment during this period, find two or three words to describe how you felt.

04. Imagine that you're living that most positive moment right now. Someone asks you how you feel. Pull together a sentence, starting 'I am . . .' or 'I feel . . .', which includes the words from Q3, or others inspired by them.

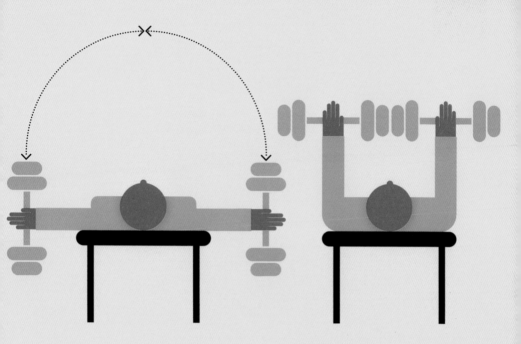

If you like what you've ended up with, you can experiment with writing these words down and/or saying them out loud on an occasional basis. You've created your own positive affirmation. It's personal to you, so you can use it as you wish.

Let's return for a moment to **Nelson Mandela. He was the first person in his family to attend secondary school. He lived his whole life immersed in a system built around the view that he was inferior. The full weight of the law and its officers would come down heavily on anyone who stepped out of line. That's a lot of** *structure* **and not a very conducive environment in which to develop a sense of** *agency.* **Yet what did he say in 1952, 42 years before it became reality? 'I shall be the first black President of South Africa.' Now THERE'S an affirmation!**

+ EXERCISE

This exercise is aimed at developing your 'reality-defining' muscles:

Write down three decisions that you're going to have to make in the next few months, for which you're hoping that this book might provide some useful clues. They don't have to be life-changing, and could in fact be quite small. Of course, in choosing which future decisions to write down, you are actually taking a decision right now. You're also creating the possibility that, as you work your way through this book, the lessons that it contains will resonate differently with you, because they'll connect with your choices. In other words, you'll have defined a different reality.

GOING WITH THE FLOW

Sometimes, it's better to decide not to decide.

Life is often written and spoken about using language that evokes the flow of a river. Work projects don't generally inspire such poetic imagery, but the parallel still applies.

Living a life, or conducting a project, could be compared to canoeing the length of a river: from the source to the delta and ultimately the sea, we'll often have to make small adjustments to stay on course. At times we may need to paddle harder in order to avoid obstacles. We may have to fight to stay above the water, or to avoid being swept away by the currents. Much of the time, though, we find ourselves simply being carried along, and in most instances that's just fine.

What's important in these latter periods is to apply relaxed acceptance and watchfulness without falling into sleepy fatalism. We don't know whether rapids, or even a waterfall, are waiting around the corner. At times, what feels like helpful momentum might actually be taking us along a dead-end tributary or in the wrong direction, and we'll have to react. But there can sometimes be real wisdom and advantage in allowing the tide to carry us and waiting to see what happens.

In business, better decision-makers often look as if they have more information at their disposal. On the sports field, better decision-makers might appear to have more time to make their own move or to intercept the opposition's. The reality, in both contexts, is that the quality of attention they've been paying to events unfolding around them *before* making their decision is such that they are able to choose the best possible moment to act; and when they do act, they've already built a clear picture of what they need to do.

The 'honeymoon' period after the appointment of a new CEO is generally seen as the time in which he or she can get away with radical decisions. Yet some of the smartest leaders I've come across have done the opposite, which is to immerse themselves in the organization without taking a position. Although his tenure as Director General of the BBC ended in political controversy, Greg Dyke's popularity with his staff, and his success in steering the corporation through the onset of the digital age, owed a lot to the fact that he spent his first few weeks sitting quietly in editing suites and local radio studios, absorbing the realities of life around this massive, dispersed institution, and conspicuously not making decisions.

The skill here is to be able to distinguish, consciously, between being in decision-making and non-decision-making mode.

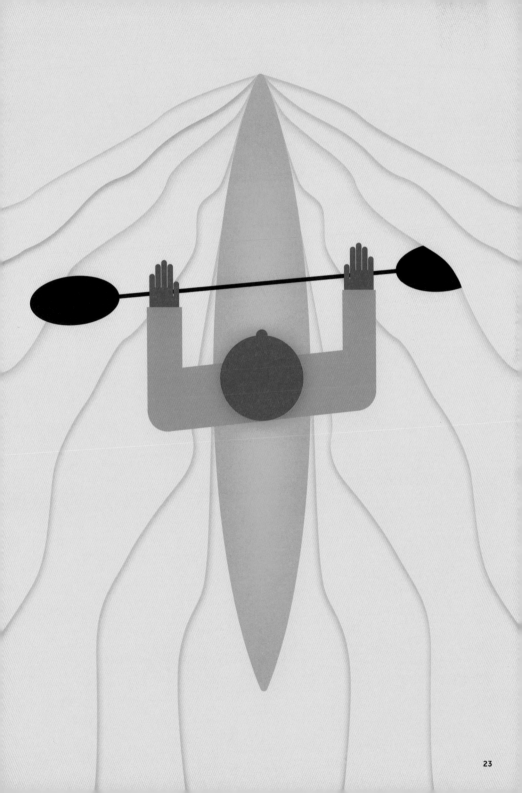

DON'T DECIDE

Shifting in and out of decision-making mode at the right moment, based on what's really going on rather than simply your preference or habits, may involve turning up your sense of agency: your belief that you can make a decision and follow it through (see Lesson 1). Or it may require you to turn up your patience in order to resist the impulse to decide.

As anyone who has ever been on a diet knows, resisting impulses is one of the hardest things for human beings to do. And when those impulses are pushing us towards something which is generally seen in a positive light – i.e. to 'be decisive' – a simple aspiration may not be enough. We may need to back it up with something more weighty, such as a solid reason why it would be better NOT to make a decision . . . yet.

At any given moment, there will be things going on in our lives in relation to which we could decide something, but which we're currently allowing to go with the flow. Identifying some of these, and the reasons behind them, can help us to make better choices about what not to decide.

There can be lots of good reasons not to make a decision. This table sets out ten. See if you can identify something in your own life (or work project) which, when you think about it, you're leaving to unfold by itself for each of them. Don't worry if you can't identify a situation for all ten. Even if just two or three come to mind, it will illustrate the fact that there are always several decisions NOT to be made.

REASON NOT TO DECIDE

- There's insufficient data
- There's conflicting data (the available signals are pointing in different directions)
- My current situation is at least as good as anything else that I could decide
- By not taking a decision, I can leave space for others to step up and take responsibility
- I don't have the resources to follow through on the decision
- There are other things that are more important right now. I should be devoting my attention to other priorities
- Other people are making a move, and I want to see what they choose to do before committing myself
- The environment is changing
- In making a decision I'll lose access to certain people / possibilities / resources
- I'm not in a good shape to make the decision; I may just be reacting or acting out my own emotions

EXAMPLE

SOMETIMES BETTER TO NOT TO DEC

IT'S
DECIDE
DE.

AN OPEN OR SHUT CASE

Would you rather be asked an open question or a closed one?

If your answer is 'open', it's already too late. That would read something along the lines of: 'What kind of question do you most like to be asked?'

My question gives you two options, so there is a decision to make, but I've determined what those options are.

If I took my lead from Thomas Hobson (1544–1631), I could restrict you even further. At its peak, Hobson's livery stable business (a kind of late-medieval car-hire equivalent) had more than 40 horses, which gave first-time customers the impression

that they would have a wide selection to choose from. But when they arrived, they were told that they could either have whichever horse was occupying the stall nearest the entrance at that moment, or no horse at all. This gave rise to the phrase 'Hobson's Choice', the equivalent of 'Take it or leave it'.

You can imagine that some people were unhappy with this. But maybe their complaints were a little unfair. In ensuring that whichever horse went out was at least fit and fresh, Hobson was protecting his customers from their own potential mistakes (after all, he knew more about what his

horses were capable of than anyone else). He was also saving the customer the time and bother involved in inspecting 40 horses, and the heartache of having to choose between them.

Sometimes, as decision-makers, we need to express a little more of our own inner Hobson. Yes, it's a fine thing to ask a big, open question: 'What are we going to do?' But, depending on the circumstances, it can be much more helpful to go with something more closed, such as 'Should we do this or should we do that?', or even the Hobsonian 'Should we do this or should we do nothing?'

An open question requires you to engage your creative faculties as well as your problem-solving ones, and involves more effort. With a closed question, a lot of the work has already been done.

As well as the nature of the challenge, judging whether to treat a decision as open or closed should take account of factors such as its importance and the time available to make it. Closed questions can generally be answered more quickly and more succinctly than open ones. Open questions invite a more thorough consideration of all the options, and reduce the chance of missing something.

IN THE FRAME

The skill that we're focusing on here is *framing*.

We're doing this all the time. Yet, just as people walking around an art gallery will rarely notice the wood or metal encasing the pictures that they're looking at, little attention is generally paid to the way in which we frame a decision.

In their article, 'The Framing of Decisions and the Psychology of Choice', Amos Tversky and Daniel Kahneman describe how changing the framing of a decision can lead us to interpret the same data in ways which result in quite different conclusions.

Depending on the nature of a decision, there may be a number of aspects which are open to reframing. As with many other approaches and techniques in this book, the way in which we actually go about this will often be the result of habits, preferences and personality traits rather than the merits of the specific case. That's why the last chapter of this book focuses on ways in which we can get to know ourselves better. When we do that, we will notice that we have a tendency to frame our decisions optimistically ('how can I get . . .') or pessimistically ('how can I avoid . . .'); or to focus on immediate steps ('what shall I do . . .') or ultimate goals ('how can I achieve . . .').

In setting the structural frame for a decision, the aim is to ensure that we're neither oversimplifying things, by asking closed questions when no clear choices are available, nor overcomplicating them, by asking open questions when clearly one of two answers will be good enough.

It's useful to be able to switch from open to closed and back again. Taking an open question and expressing it as a closed one can be a short cut through lots of information. Taking a closed question and reframing it as an open one can reveal new possibilities, and demonstrate that you are less constrained than you might have thought.

In Lesson 1, you were invited to identify three decisions – big or small – that you are going to have to make in the next few months. Are you able to express them in both open and closed forms?

	OPEN	CLOSED
EXAMPLES	What shall I do?	Shall I do X or Y?
	Where should I go?	Should I go to A, B or C?
Decision 1		
Decision 2		
Decision 3		

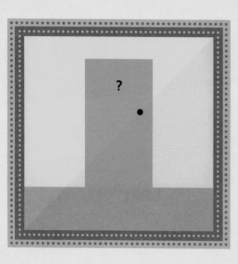 

Once you've grasped both approaches, you can start to mix them up – e.g. by drawing a Decision Tree like the one below, which helps to set about framing your decision.

HOW MANY POTENTIAL ANSWERS ARE THERE?			
FEW		**MANY**	
Are the options clear or unclear?		**Define open question**	
Clear	Unclear	Brainstorm potential answers	
Define closed question	List the options	Group potential answers	
	Assess the options	**How many groups are there?**	
		Few	Many
		Define closed question	Assess the options
⋮	⋮	⋮	⋮
↓	↓	↓	↓
DECIDE	**DECIDE**	**DECIDE**	**DECIDE**

MAKE OR TAKE

Taking a decision is different from *making* a decision.

Taking a decision happens at a particular moment. Making a decision can last minutes, hours, weeks, or even years. Making a decision is a process, which has a start, a middle and an end point. The end point is to *take* a decision. That's why most of the lessons in this book are about the things we can do *before* we take a decision.

We take hundreds of decisions every day. Many of these are routine or unimportant, which is fortunate, as we could never have enough time to make them all. But when faced with decisions that matter, or are complex, it's a natural response to pause for thought. This suggests an innate understanding that the more we are able to shift from taking decisions to making them, the better they will be.

It's true that once a decision has been taken, there may still be opportunities to adjust, or to change our mind. Yet most decisions involve cutting off alternative possibilities. In saying 'yes' to one thing, we're saying 'no' to others.

Sometimes, by committing to a decision, we're *killing off* all other options. Strong language? Yes, but also precise. The word 'decision' comes from the same root as incision: 'cut'; and 'decide' is related to suicide and pesticide: 'kill'. No wonder so many of us hesitate when confronted with an important decision: the knife with which we cut away unwanted options can feel as if it's hanging over our own head.

Any chef will tell you that when it comes to knives, a sharp one is not just more effective than a dull one, it's safer. Why? Because you're more likely to treat a sharp knife with respect. And because you don't have to hack away and risk a messy slip. Good chefs look after their knives, and generally carry their own set with them.

The skills required to make and take better decisions are similarly personal and portable. The ideas and techniques offered in this book are designed to help you develop a fuller, sharper set of tools to carry with you. They should be equally useful as you face small, everyday choices and major, life-affecting forks in the road.

SAYING 'NO' TO SAY 'YES'

Making a decision is like making a sculpture. There are two basic directions in which you can move towards the finished article: the additive and the subtractive.

Most modern sculptors use an *additive* process, where materials are assembled, or poured into a cast. Traditional sculptors use a *subtractive* method, where they chip away and remove material – usually stone or wood – in order to 'reveal' the finished article. As you watch the subtractive sculptor at work, you will see a human form, a horse, whatever their subject is, emerge from the block of marble or oak, while a pile of discarded chunks and shavings builds up below.

Most of the decision-making ideas and techniques in this book could be described as additive. They involve assembling and organizing data, opinions, ideas and other material in order to construct a decision. But we can sometimes get to the 'yes' of a decision more quickly by adopting a subtractive process and chipping away the 'no' elements.

You could describe this as a process of elimination. It's similar to an approach employed by detectives, and was summed up by one of the most famous fictional exponents of that trade, Sherlock Holmes: *'How often have I said to you that when you have eliminated the impossible, whatever remains, however improbable, must be the truth?' (The Sign of Four)*

Of course, a fully scientific approach to this would involve listing all the available theories before starting to eliminate them. But even Holmes wasn't immune to trusting his more intuitive faculties at times. We have other forms of intelligence at our disposal in addition to the straightforwardly logical; one

of the easiest ways to access some of these is simply to speed things up and let go of any need to be precise or to justify what we come up with.

Identify a decision, and imagine that you're going to be held to it. Let's say that someone has made you an offer: that you can celebrate your next birthday in any way you wish (expense not a barrier), on the condition that you come up with a clear description of what you want to do.

Rather than thinking about what you might like to ask for, let's start with six 'no's – things you don't want – and then jump to a 'yes'. The trick is to write the seven answers down as quickly as you can, without worrying whether they make sense or not. After all, you're in the process of discarding six of them.

NO	I don't want . . .
NO	I don't want . . .
NO	I don't want . . .
NO	I don't want . . .
NO	I don't want . . .
NO	I don't want . . .
YES	I DO want . . .

Try the same technique again, with one or two real decisions that you have to make right now or in the future. Even if your first intuitive 'yes' doesn't feel right, a few minutes spent examining what you've cut out of the equation with your 'no's could point you in the direction of the choice that you do want to make.

TOOLKIT

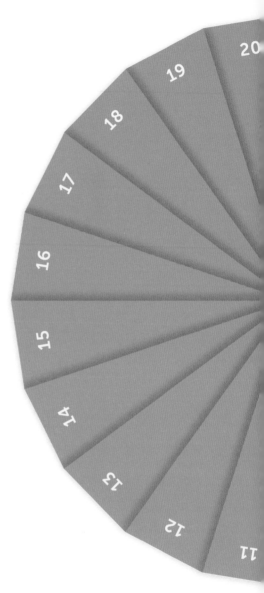

01

Making decisions and following them through requires us to have a sense of 'agency'. While there may be some externally generated limits to this, a lot depends on our own confidence levels, and these can be built over time.

02

Sometimes it's better *not to* make a decision. We may not have enough information yet, or things may be unfolding in a helpful way without us needing to decide. When we're not in decision-making mode, staying alert to what's going on around us will mean that we're better equipped to make a decision when we do need to.

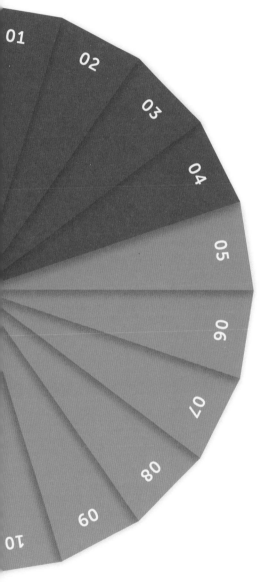

03

How you frame a decision can make it easier or harder to arrive at a conclusion, and can increase or decrease the chances of making a good call. Understanding your own default or habitual approach is important. Then you can choose to go a different way, if that will achieve a better result.

04

Making a decision usually involves shutting down some options. Sometimes it helps to start by thinking about what you *don't* want, before arriving at the moment when you take your decision.

FURTHER LEARNING

READ

Who Do We Choose To Be?
Margaret Wheatley (Berrett-Koehler, 2017)

Synchronicity: The Inner Path of Leadership
Joseph Jaworski (Berrett-Koehler, 2011)

Leadership is an Art
Max De Pree (Bantam Doubleday Dell, 1990)

LISTEN

Letter to My Daughter (Audiobook)
Dr Maya Angelou

WATCH

A Simple Trick to Improve Positive Thinking
Alison Ledgerwood, TEDx Talk

The Power of Vulnerability
Brené Brown, TED Talk

THE SHAPE OF A DECISION

LESSONS

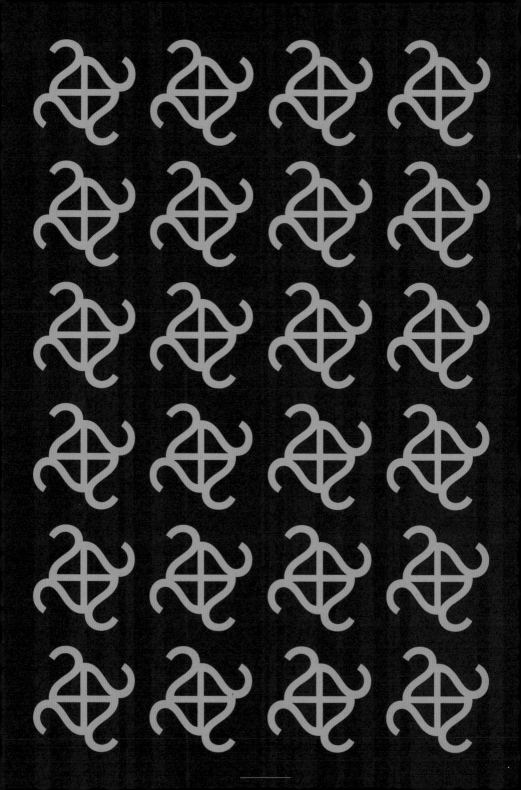

The relevant data to help us make our decision won't just fall into our laps. We need to seek it out.

It may appear logical to suggest that effectiveness in decision-making equates to being 'decisive'. But decisiveness implies leaping to conclusions, and that's actually the opposite of what a great decision-maker does.

This is a big claim, so to back it up let's get the view of one of the greatest decision-makers of all time, Albert Einstein:

'If I had an hour to solve a problem and my life depended on the solution, I would spend the first 55 minutes determining the proper question to ask, for once I know the proper question, I could solve the problem in less than five minutes.'

Einstein had a prodigious work ethic, so he's not suggesting that we should simply gaze out of the window, hoping for enlightenment to strike. There's serious work to be done during those first 55 minutes, or whatever represents the bulk of the time available for a decision, which might be seconds, weeks or months.

The relevant data to help us make our decision won't just fall into our laps. We need to seek it out. Once we've got it, we need to organize and analyze it, to see where it's pointing us.

When the stakes are high, embarking on these tasks can feel like taking a detour into territory where there's a risk of getting distracted or losing our way entirely. So what we need is a map, to reassure ourselves that we really are heading towards a reliable solution.

This chapter provides that reassurance by tracing the shape of a decision. After an initial overview (Lesson 5), we'll take a detailed look at three elements. Lesson 6 encourages us to suspend judgement as we collect data. Lesson 7 invites us to push the data around and see what it shows us, before – finally – we arrive at the moment of choice (Lesson 8). Once you're familiar with these steps, the sequence should come so naturally that you'll achieve Einsteinian levels of assurance.

THE WHOLE PROCESS

Decisions vary hugely in their nature and content. However, it is possible to identify a single shape that can help, whether you're making small, everyday decisions, or major, life-changing ones. It can guide you through a fifteen-minute agenda item in a team meeting; an hour-long presentation to a potential client; a three-month exploration of career options; a major organization change programme; or a family chat about what colour to paint the living room.

The shape is inspired by a simple, three-stage process map which can be used to describe how almost anything is made:

Inputs	Throughputs	Outputs
···>	···>	···>
Raw Materials	**Manufacturing Process**	**Finished Product**

Yet our decision-making process is more than just a straight line. Yes, it will ideally have a defined starting point (a question or challenge), and reach a clear destination, but in between it needs to create a space to explore information and ideas before bringing us safely to our decision.

Represented graphically, it looks something like this: **< = >**

Each of the elements provides a strong visual clue as to what that step is about, and how to approach it.

< has a single starting point, then opens up so that we can populate it with data to inform our decision-making.

= keeps the space open for us to examine the data and see what it tells us without jumping to conclusions, but also maintains boundaries to stop us straying too far from the task at hand.

> invites us to eliminate some options and to narrow in on a clear conclusion.

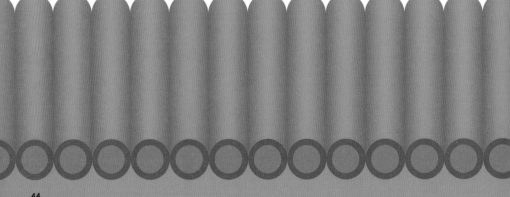

Technically, the three steps can be described as Divergent (<), Emergent (=) and Convergent (>). Yet it's probably more memorable and useful to identify them through the questions and activities that relate to each of them:

< WHAT?

What are the facts, the ideas and the contextual factors that will inform the decision?

The activity here is *Collecting,* which involves bringing as much data as possible into the equation.

= SO WHAT?

So what are the themes, inter-relationships and priorities that show up in the data?

The activity is *Considering,* which involves sorting and evaluating the data, looking for patterns and weighing up potential consequences.

> NOW WHAT?

Now what are the conclusions and the decision?

The activity is *Choosing.*

Together they form a single process, but each step requires different skills and energy.

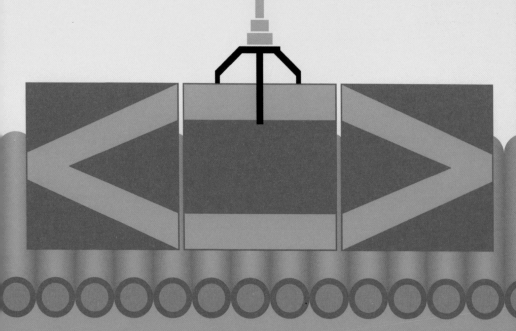

THREE STEPS TO A DECISION

Much of the power of this process lies in the fact that it reflects what most of us do quite naturally, given the time and space. To test this, think about a decision that you've made in the last few weeks and describe it using the three steps.

I NEEDED TO DECIDE . . .		
First, I . . .	< (collected)	
Then I . . .	= (considered)	
Finally, I . . .	> (chose)	

Now, see if you can use the whole process to make a new decision. Imagine that you have been asked to sum up the quality that you find most admirable in people. Give just one or two minutes to each step.

< **Write down the names of eight people you really admire (whether you know them personally or not).**

= **Look at the names you've written down.** For each one, come up with a single word to describe what it is that you most admire about that person. Write these words on eight separate pieces of paper. See if you can organize any similar words into pairs or clusters; physically group them together, and consider whether a name suggests itself for any of the groupings. Now rank them, placing the ones that you consider most important at the top and those that matter less at the bottom.

> **Revisit the question:** 'What quality do you find most admirable in people?' Look at your responses to the last stage. You may be drawn to the word that comes up most often, or that summarizes the biggest cluster of related words. Maybe there's another word that you feel answers the question best. Perhaps it's the one that's at the top of your ranking. Make your choice!

You might feel that you could have leapt straight to an answer and saved yourself the time and effort involved in the first two stages. It's hard to prove whether or not you would have come up with exactly the same quality. What is clear, though, is that having gone through the whole process, you're much better equipped to explain or defend your choice if called upon to do so.

When you've worked through all the stages in the following three lessons, why not return to both of these exercises? Is there a bigger or more complex past decision that you're able to describe using the three steps? Then revisit the question of the quality that you find most admirable in people and see whether what you've learned affects your ultimate decision, or the way in which you approach the question.

< WHAT?

Greater choice is generally seen as a desirable thing, but that's not always the case. Just ask anyone who has wasted half of what was supposed to be a relaxed evening, scrolling through 300 movies on their TV subscription service.

Choice requires effort, whereas certainty conserves energy. This is one reason why, even when the stakes are high, we're so keen to narrow down the number of options in front of us as quickly as possible.

But narrowing our options means we could be missing the most interesting and fruitful ways forward. The *What?* phase of decision-making guards against this by opening up possibilities.

A classic *What?* methodology is brainstorming, where the instruction that there's 'no such thing as a bad idea' is designed to counter our impulse to leap immediately to conclusions.

Yet the *What?* phase isn't just concerned with the capturing of knowledge and the generation of ideas. It also provides an opportunity to surface assumptions and bring our feelings into the equation. Whether working alone or in a team, the most potent enemy of an effective *What?* process is judgement. What we believe, what we're afraid of, or what we really want might be pivotal considerations as we move towards our decision. These factors are likely to be driving us whether we're aware of them or not, so it makes sense to bring them out into the open.

As well as looking inside ourselves, it's important to notice what's going on around us that could contribute to our decision. When we exclaim something along the lines of 'the answer was staring me in the face all the time', we're acknowledging that a more complete examination of the facts and circumstances would have told us what to do next. Wise leaders will regularly 'walk the floor', asking their team members open questions about what's going on. Successful projects often start with stakeholder interviews, or 'learning journeys', where the objective is simply to see the reality of the current situation.

In environments such as the military, or elite sport outfits, where high-stakes decisions have to be made quickly, significant emphasis is also put on capturing as much information as possible about what has already happened. This may take the form of an After Action Review or Situation Report. The rationale here is that, in order to learn about the future, and to try to shape it through effective decisions, it helps to have a comprehensive view of both the past and the present.

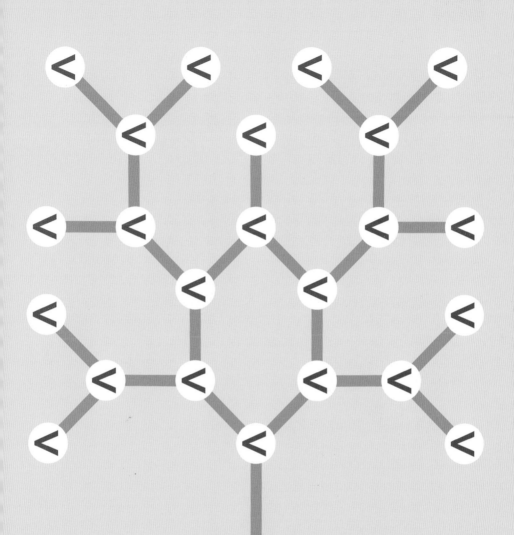

BRINGING IN THE HARVEST

The word 'data' literally means 'what is given'.

So it makes sense that the skills required to be effective at the *What?* phase are more about gathering in what already exists than generating something new. *What?* time is harvest time.

Even in unfamiliar territory, it would be unusual for there to be no data available to help you. Choose one of the three decisions that you identified at the end of Lesson 1. Now see if you can come up with at least one item under each of these headings that might impact your decision.

Facts What I know	
Assumptions / Opinions What I believe	
Emotions What I feel	
Context What's going on	
Ideas What could work	

As you do this, you may notice two impulses. The first is to immediately evaluate or assess what you've come up with. This is to be resisted, for now at least. The second is to keep going, creating longer lists under some of the headings. This is to be encouraged, as you're looking to get as much data as possible into your frame.

Looking at past experiences can be another rich source of material, but there's a risk of it being distorted, based on whether or not the central objective was met. In sport or the military, if the match or battle was won, the tendency will be to overemphasize the upside, and to downplay mistakes. If it was lost, the tasks that were carried out effectively, which might contribute to future success, could be ignored.

To avoid these pitfalls, many teams and organizations conduct After Action Reviews using a standard format, which separates:

Think about the last time you went on a holiday. By answering the four questions from the After Action Review, you may not come up with the ideal plan for your next break, but you'll probably land on some potent clues.

If family or friends accompanied you on that last holiday, and you ask them the same questions, you may bump into differences of substance or emphasis in their responses. At the *What?* stage, this is a plus: it provides more material for you to work with, and nobody's opinion should take precedence over anyone else's. Even the most hierarchical organizations (such as the military) will often suspend the privileges of rank during an After Action Review. This acknowledges the fact that the most junior member of the team may have had the best view or insight into what happened, while the most senior may have been least aware.

What was expected / intended to happen? from **What actually happened?**
and then asks: **What went wrong and why?**
and finally, **What went well and why?**

CHOICE RE
EFFORT, W
CERTAINTY
ENERGY.

QUIRES
HEREAS
ONSERVES

⹀ SO WHAT?

During the *What?* phase, the aim is to assemble as much data as possible before you start analyzing it. But human beings are always looking for patterns, so it's natural to feel an urge to move beyond the simple collection of data and to find yourself wanting to organize it into themes and hierarchies.

Now you can surrender to this impulse. It's time to 'consider' the information you have collected and to search for meaning. But you haven't yet reached the moment when you need to make a firm choice, so you can still afford to try things out.

It's tempting to see *So What?* as a process of arithmetic, or even more narrowly, accountancy: you simply organize your data into columns, assess the costs and benefits, and choose the option with the greatest number of ticks and the fewest crosses.

This kind of approach can work. But by looking more closely for the connections *between* the different items in your columns, what you're aiming to do is identify threads of meaning amongst the data that you've collected, and to weave those threads into a coherent narrative, which will lead to the threshold of a decision.

As you embark on this process, you don't know what insights it will generate. Hence the 'emergent' description in Lesson 5. What you do have – built into you – is a deep capacity to spot connections and construct narratives. As human beings, one of our superpowers is meaning-making, and we do this through telling stories and engaging in conversation.

This is beautifully explained by Theodore Zeldin, in his book *Conversation*:

'Conversation is a meeting of minds with different memories and habits. When minds meet, they don't just exchange facts: they transform them, reshape them, draw different implications from them, engage in new trains of thought. Conversation doesn't just reshuffle the cards: it creates new cards.'

We may or may not have the opportunity – during our decision-making process – to engage in conversation with other people. What we can do, even if we're working alone, is to take a conversational approach, by adopting a number of different viewpoints in relation to the same challenge, in order to consider it from all angles.

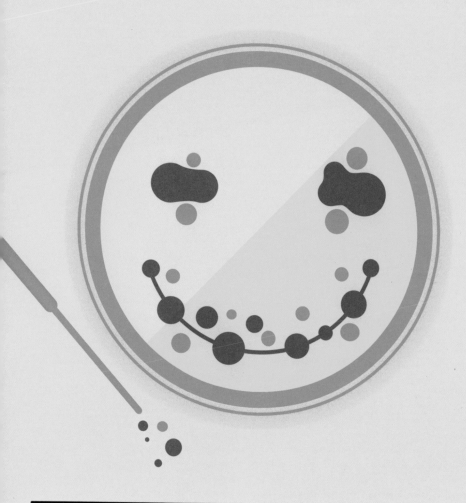

The post-it note is the ultimate *So What?* tool. In order for something to be genuinely 'emergent', you need to be able to experiment with it, which means moving things around and holding back from reaching a definitive conclusion. The post-it note is itself the product of an emergent discovery process. The glue that makes it possible was invented, accidentally, in 1968 by Spencer Silver (he was trying to create a super-strong bonding material). It wasn't until six years later that his colleague at 3M, Art Fry, who sang in a local church choir, came up with the idea of using the weak but resilient adhesive on small pieces of paper, so that he could mark the pages of his hymn book without damaging them.

NAVIGATING COMPLEXITIES

Whether you use sticky bits of paper, a spreadsheet or a sketch book, it's important to organize your data so that as much of it as possible is visible to you at the same time. This is because the key to unlocking your decision may only become apparent when you see the whole picture.

Occasionally, you might find that you have a bunch of arrows all pointing towards the same conclusion. In such cases, it's still worth investing a little time to check for the complexities which might be hidden at the margins or intersections.

Simplicity is about unbroken straight lines, whereas complexity is full of twists, turns and jumps. Reading a complex situation is much easier once you understand the different forms it may take, as categorized by Peter Senge and his fellow pioneers in their 'Fifth Discipline' model:

- **Social Complexity.** The problem that you're addressing involves different stakeholders with different agendas and ideas.
- **Generative Complexity.** The problem is new, and is still evolving.
- **Dynamic Complexity.** Cause and effect are separated from each other in time or space, so your decision may bring unintended consequences.

Assessing the different ways in which a challenge might be complex can be achieved by asking some headline questions. If the answers suggest that a particular form of complexity is present, then it may be worth undertaking a further activity to explore how things could play out. You'll also get a clue as to what kind of approach to adopt as you implement your decision.

Complexity is the glitch between cause and effect, and the undoing of many overconfident decision-makers, who expect the world to behave in a linear, predictable way. But in life's game of Snakes & Ladders, which can see a wrong move punished by slipping back to your starting point (or worse), complexity can also be the ladder up which you can access hidden assets and unlock new possibilities.

TYPE OF COMPLEXITY	HEADLINE QUESTIONS	WORTH FURTHER CONSIDERATION IF . . .	FURTHER ACTIVITIES
Social Complexity	Who has an interest in this? Who's affected? What does person / group X, Y, Z think and want?	Person / group X, Y or Z have different interests, perspectives or priorities	Stakeholder mapping; Venn diagram to identify overlapping priorities; maintaining an inclusive approach
Generative Complexity	What other models / examples can we learn from?	Nothing fits the bill	Defining what success looks like; maintaining a visionary approach
Dynamic Complexity	What happens if . . . ? How do the key factors interrelate?	Lots of unpredictability; delayed reactions and / or knock-on effects	Systems map / decision tree; maintaining a holistic approach

Try the questions above in relation to one of your prospective decisions from Lesson 1, and see if you can identify which form(s) of complexity might apply.

Potential conclusions are bound to come up during the *So What?* phase. Indeed, that's what we're looking for. But it's important to hold these lightly, while maintaining a sense of curiosity to explore further. It will help if we label anything that comes up at this stage as a hypothesis. Once we're confident that we've considered as much of the data as possible within the available time, we can move on and ask: *Now What?*

> NOW WHAT?

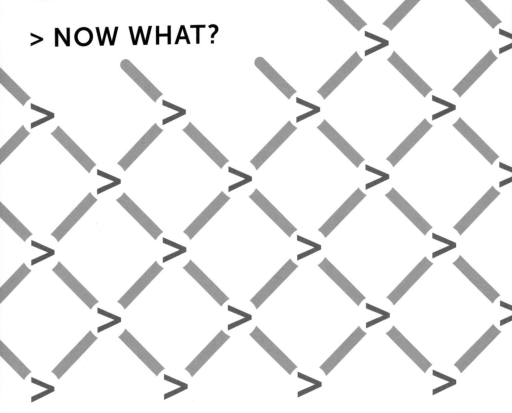

At this point, the decision-maker becomes a decision-taker.

As the shape demonstrates, the > *Now What?* phase is the opposite of < *What?* There, we wanted to collect as much material as possible. Here, it's about eliminating options to arrive at our ultimate choice.

One extreme, but illuminating, method of doing this was pioneered by George Cockcroft, better known by his pen-name, Luke Rhinehart, who experimented with making choices by rolling a dice. Cockcroft claims that this is how he met his wife. He was driving home one day when he spotted two nurses waiting for a bus. He got out his dice. If an odd number came up, he would offer them a lift. One of them was Ann, and at the time of telling this story, they had been married for more than 60 years.

Although he could hardly come from a more different historical context, Cockcroft/ Rhinehart's approach might have been met with approval from the twelfth-century scholar Maimonides, who asserted that 'the risk of a wrong decision is preferable to the terror of indecision'. The spirit of Maimonides lives on in the management trope advanced by, among others, Richard Branson: that 'a bad decision is often better than no decision'.

At the end of well-executed *What?* and *So What?* phases, the decision-maker will often realize that they already 'know' what their choice will be. If that's not the case, and several potential options remain, then narrowing in on a decision through a process of elimination (Lesson 4) can clarify things. Here, the 'accountancy' approach, which was unhelpful during *So What?*, comes into its own. But now you have the assurance of knowing that your list of options, and the pros and cons that you set alongside each one, are based on a fuller consideration of the situation's possibilities and complexities.

Perhaps the most important quality to bring to *Now What?* is clarity of expression. Even if an important decision is one that only you need to know about, it can still make sense to put it on the record: to mark the end of the decision-making process, and to capture what has been decided. If others are involved, the wording of the minutes, or the email that you send out afterwards, actually becomes the decision. The effectiveness of a team is as likely to be affected by their levels of shared understanding and clarity about what has been decided as it is by whether what they're doing represents the best option.

ACTION HEROES

A café in the heart of one of Paris's most fashionable districts may seem an unlikely place to find not just one, but two action heroes. Yet, in the 1950s, if you wanted an audience with Simone de Beauvoir or Jean-Paul Sartre, the first place to look was Les Deux Magots, and if that failed, you could always try Café Flore next door.

As the mother and father (or trendy aunt and uncle) of Existentialism, Sartre and de Beauvoir asserted that human beings define themselves through their choices, and that even not choosing is a choice. Humans are 'condemned to be free', and are therefore 'responsible for everything [they do]'. They have to face up to the consequences of their choices, both for themselves and for others.

In this respect, we're not just the director of our own movie, we're the scriptwriter too. Most importantly, for Sartre and de Beauvoir, we're also the actor, because nothing is more important than what we choose to *do*.

Whether or not you agree that our choices define us, it's hard to argue with the view that every decision represents an attempt to shape events and influence circumstances or people. However, this cannot apply if the decision in question consists solely of an inner resolution, or even something that we say, or is recorded in the minutes of a meeting. Sartre summarized this with typical economy: *'Commitment is an act, not a word.'*

Although we might use different language, many of us will recognize the truth of this. It's a common occurrence that a decision to do, or to change something, can appear to have been made and agreed inside a room, only for everyone to leave and then carry on doing things in exactly the same way as before. The temptation in such a case is to complain that people are going against the decision, but it's probably more accurate to say that, until the decision becomes visible through action, it hasn't really been taken at all. The same applies to all those personal resolutions, which never quite translate into what we actually eat for lunch, or how many times we get to the gym.

So the advice here is simple: 'cooling off' periods are very useful when we've been confronted with taking a major decision at short notice. But if we've managed to do the < *What?* and the = *So What?* before our final > *Now What?*, and if we then have the opportunity to take immediate action, that can be the most effective way of completing our decision.

Kurt Vonnegut came up with one of the best-known (and best) jokes about philosophy:

'To be is to do' **Socrates**

'To do is to be' **Sartre**

'Do Be Do Be Do' **Sinatra**

TOOLKIT

05

Making a decision involves collecting data,
considering what it means, then choosing
how to move forwards. Whether we have
a few seconds or a few months to make a
decision, it pays to divide our time and effort
across these three steps.

06

When we take the time to look around us,
or to think about our decision, we'll usually
find that a considerable amount of data
is available. Collecting as much of this as
possible, while resisting the urge to evaluate
or interpret it, provides the foundation for a
good decision.

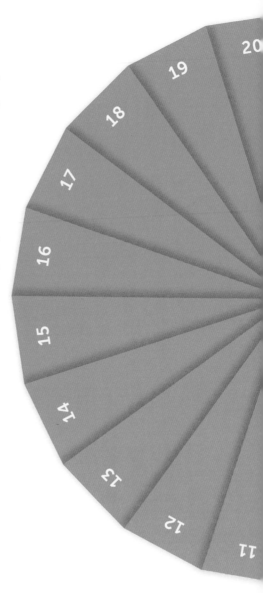

07

When we start to organize and consider the data we've uncovered, we will often see patterns and themes which might point to our ultimate decision. Welcoming and understanding complexities can help us to identify short-cuts to the right answer, or to avoid unintended consequences.

08

When we ultimately take a decision, it's important to articulate it as clearly as possible (even if only to ourselves), and to follow it up with meaningful action. Until we've done this, it could be argued that no decision has really been taken.

FURTHER LEARNING

READ

'The Ladder of Inference' by Chris Argyris in
The Fifth Discipline
Peter Senge (Penguin Random House, 2006)

Conversation
Theodore Zeldin (The Harvill Press, 1998)

Six Thinking Hats
Edward de Bono (1985; Penguin, 2009)

Edward de Bono designed a system of six 'thinking hats', each representing a distinct orientation, which might offer a different view of both a challenge and possible solutions. The White Hat relates to the facts of the matter; the Yellow Hat symbolizes brightness and optimism, and invites an exploration of the positives. The Black Hat is the Devil's Advocate, which looks for the pitfalls and dangers of things going wrong. The Red Hat encourages the decision-maker to bring feelings, hunches and intuition – her own and others' – into the equation. The Green Hat represents creativity, and asks whether new concepts might be part of the solution. The Blue Hat relates to process: organizing and planning for action.

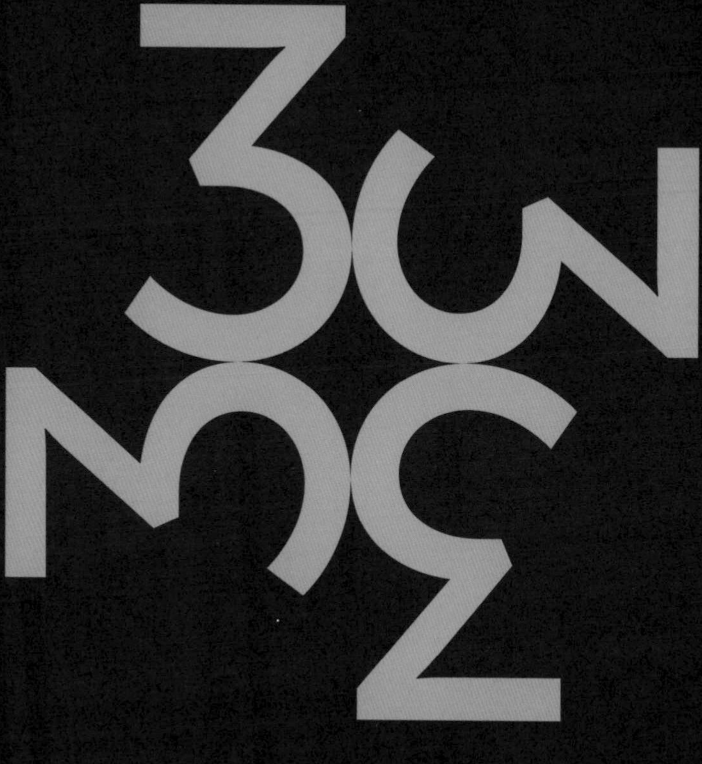

STRATEGIZING

LESSONS

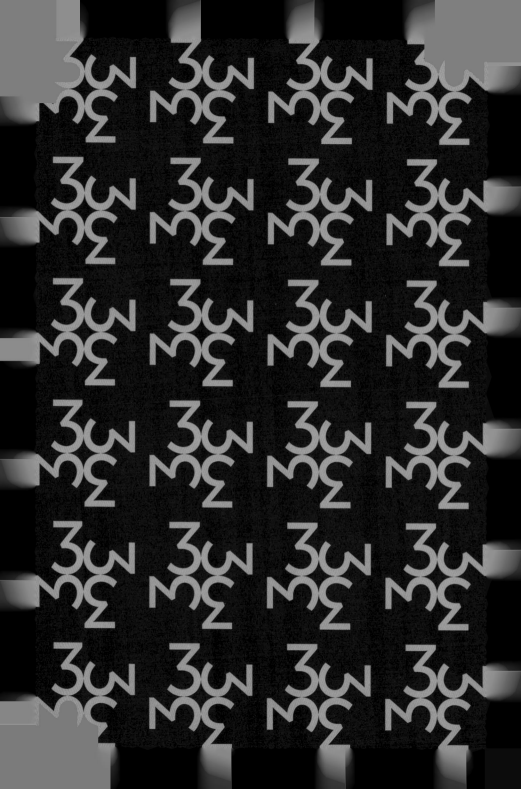

Strategizing is the act of zooming out to see the bigger picture, but also zooming in to examine the details.

In the late 1990s, the *Guardian* newspaper ran a TV advert which featured the same scene shot from three different angles. In the first, we see a skinhead appearing to run away from a car, as if he's being attacked; in the second, shot from behind him, we see that he is running towards a man, as if about to attack him; in the third – a wider shot – we see that he has sprinted to help the man out of harm's way, as a load of bricks drops from a hoist. The punchline is: 'It's only when you get the whole picture that you can fully understand what's going on.'

Strategizing is the act of zooming out to see the bigger picture, but also zooming in to examine the details. It's the golfer, crouching in three or four different spots to see the green's contours before putting; it's the mountain guide, checking the weather forecast and the level of wear on her ropes before setting out; it's the parents, studying the transport links and the state of the local schools before deciding in which neighbourhood to make their new home. Tactics are about things. Strategizing is about the relationships between things.

In this chapter, we're going to examine strategizing itself from three different angles: above (astronomy) in Lesson 9, below (archaeology) in Lesson 10, and laterally (geography) in Lesson 11, before pulling our own camera back in Lesson 12 to see how an appreciation of 'the whole' can help with your decision-making.

What this chapter won't attempt to do is pin down what 'strategy' is. There are enough books about that already, and if you read five of them at random, you'll probably be confronted with five different definitions.

We're more concerned with the verb than the noun. A better decision-maker may or may not have an explicit strategy. What she does have is the ability to *strategize*.

ASTRONOMY

'The fox knows many things, but the hedgehog knows one big thing.'
Greek poet Archilochus (c. 680–645 BC)

The differing approaches of the fox and the hedgehog are based on the opportunities and challenges arising from their physical characteristics and the terrain in which they operate.

Hedgehogs are only capable of eating what's under their nose: worms, caterpillars, and so on. Being unable to outpace the creatures that might aspire to eat *them* (such as birds of prey and – yes – foxes), their defence routine is to curl themselves into a ball, with their sharp quills protecting them. And wherever they are – be it town or countryside – hedgehogs will adopt more or less the same behaviour.

Foxes, on the other hand, will change their diet, their sleeping patterns and even their levels of 'shyness' or willingness to engage with other animals (such as humans), depending on the context.

The hedgehog has a strategy, but the fox is a strategist.

People are natural strategists too, but unlike foxes or hedgehogs, we want and need more than food, rest and safety. Perhaps the best-known description of this is to be found in

the 'Hierarchy of Needs', published in 1943 by the American psychologist Abraham Maslow. He acknowledges that 'physiological' and 'safety' considerations come before anything else, but goes on to point out that love and belonging, esteem and achievement are also essential ingredients for a healthy, happy life.

At the top of Maslow's Hierarchy is the fulfilment of our potential, which he calls self-actualization. We humans are explorers and achievers. We're always looking for meaning and direction. When we have these two things, life can feel straightforward. When they're missing, we can feel lost. 'Where am I going?' and 'Why does this

matter?' are questions which are not confined to philosophers, but come up for most of us from time to time.

This is handy, because they're great questions to ask as we make any kind of decision. In directing our attention beyond what's in front of our nose, they challenge us to 'be less hedgehog and more fox'. They invite us into the bigger picture and are therefore fundamentally strategic.

There's also the risk that these questions could feel vague and disorientate us. Fortunately, though, we're well equipped to navigate our way through big questions: all we have to do is look at the stars.

FIND YOUR NORTH STAR

If you were designing a planet, and knew its inhabitants would wish to move around it, you could do a lot worse than stick a big arrow in the sky, which always pointed in the same direction. That's exactly what Polaris – or the North Star – does, and for thousands of years it has helped humans find their way.

In decision-making, having a North Star means knowing where you're heading. You can find your North Star by asking questions such as 'What am I trying to achieve?' or 'Where am I trying to get to?'

These questions open up the bigger picture, but may also set a trap for the strategist. There are many things you *could*

be trying to achieve, and many places you *could* be trying to reach. Choosing the wrong one would be like using Sirius – the Dog Star – as your guide rather than the North Star. Sirius is much easier to spot than Polaris, but because of the earth's rotation, it is constantly in motion relative to the horizon, so depending on when you look, it will point you in a completely different direction.

One way to check that you've found the real, astronomical North Star, is to look for the seven stars forming the recognizable constellation – known in the UK as The Plough, and in North America as The Big

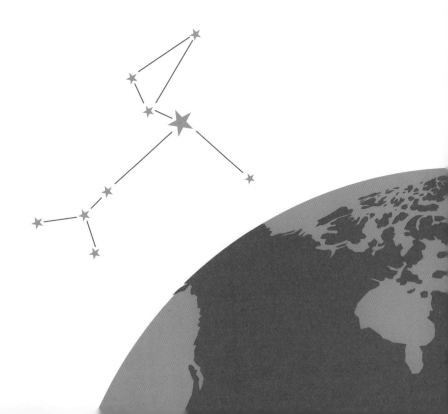

Dipper – which points reliably to Polaris.

For the careful strategist, a way of checking that your own North Star can be relied upon is to see whether it aligns with your inner constellation of deeper priorities and motivations.

This can be done by asking '5 Whys'. You simply take your response to the headline question, and then ask: 'Why does that matter?' And when you've generated the answer to that question, you ask the same again: 'Why does *that* (the new answer) matter?' 'And why does *that* matter? . . . and *that*? . . . and *that*?'

If you run out of steam before the fifth 'why?', it may be that your original answer doesn't deserve 'North Star' status, and you may find a stronger articulation of your headline objective in your response to another of the 'whys?'.

Ultimately, you'll find that you can lock in on the destination you really want to get to, or at least your direction of travel. But reaching for the stars without having a clear sense of the ground you're standing on can cause all sorts of problems. So the strategist's next job is to dig: not like a farmer or a builder might dig, but more carefully, like an archaeologist, with a view to examining and learning from whatever is revealed.

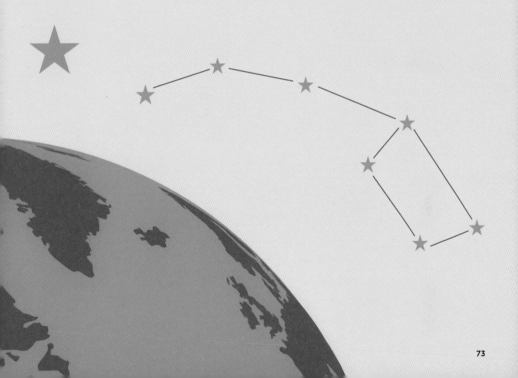

ARCHAEOLOGY

If a fox, under attack by a powerful dog, decided to mimic a hedgehog's defence and curl itself into a ball, the outcome would be swift and bloody.

The effective strategist understands the true nature and capabilities of the protagonist (the organization, team or individual whose job it will be to implement a strategy), and makes decisions that are a good fit. This doesn't just apply to obvious characteristics, which can – in any case – grow, diminish or change over time. It's also about the protagonist's deeper purpose, patterns and instincts. And the best way to study these is to dig into the past, which is what's involved in the practice of archaeology.

As with many famous 'quotations', it seems that Henry Ford never actually uttered the precise statement, 'History is bunk', although he did say something to that effect, counselling specifically against getting caught up in tradition. Another Ford quote, however, demonstrates that he was keenly interested in the two different kinds of history that should be key considerations for an effective strategist and decision-maker.

When he said that his customers could have a car 'painted any colour, so long as it's black', Ford was respecting his company's *heritage*, which was built on standardization, functionality and production quality. He was also rejecting the tendency of his sales team to pay too much attention to passing trends.

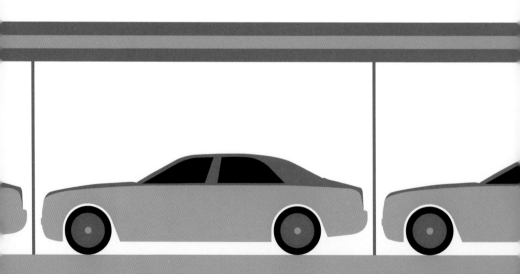

In his view, this was an example of *baggage*, associated with the history and culture of the sales function.

Heritage is anything that you've acquired, learned, been through or built that might be useful to you in facing your current challenge. Heritage can also relate to the feelings that attach themselves to those positive assets, such as confidence. Heritage may be earned through blood and toil, or inherited by chance. The point is, it's there; it's in the bank and it can help.

Baggage is what history has left us that could hold us back. It's the memories of past failures; the fault-lines in relationships. It may include capabilities or assumptions which were helpful once, but are now past their 'use-by' date. For example, that underdog mentality which drove us to the top might actually hold us back now that we're trying to stay there.

Left hidden, baggage can cause us to misread a situation. And if we're not aware of our heritage, we may underestimate our capabilities, or act in a way that cuts across our own interests. Just as the archaeologist knows that digging deeper might reveal greater treasures and perhaps shed light on contemporary issues, so the strategist understands that, by studying their own history and origins, or those of the team on whose behalf a decision will be made, they will find valuable clues to inform their decision.

HERITAGE AND BAGGAGE

A magical thing, which happens when the strategist gets to work, is that the benefits of studying the bigger picture can be unlocked *just by asking the question* and seeing which answers immediately suggest themselves.

✛EXERCISE

Dig out your own heritage and baggage as a decision-maker. Draw a line down the middle of a page. Write 'Heritage' at the top of one column and 'Baggage' at the top of the other. Think about your track record in making decisions: the times when things have or haven't worked out the way you wished, and see if you can come up with three or four items under each heading.

Now consider your answers, and ask yourself:

- What kind of decision-maker am I?
- What advantages have I got going for me, and what could hold me back in making good decisions?

Heritage	Baggage

Now try a more specific version of the same exercise, focusing on one of the imminent decisions that you identified in Lesson 1. When you think about that decision, what positive and negative memories and feelings come up from past experience? List them under the 'Heritage' and 'Baggage' headings.

Often, it will be enough just to notice what you've got going for you, and what might be holding you back. In many religious and spiritual traditions, the key to casting out ghosts or demons is simply to name them, and particularly on the 'Baggage' side of the equation, just acknowledging what's there could be pivotal.

Other elements that come up might affect your decision more directly. You may need to identify actions to exploit aspects of your heritage, or to 'repair' or work around your baggage. If this is the case, the specific points can be incorporated into the analytical processes set out in Lessons 11 and 12, and factored into your decision-making.

This archaeological exploration dovetails with the astronomical approach of Lesson 9. If you've tested your North Star by working through the '5 Whys', you should notice that the personal motivations and values, which came into focus as you described your desired destination, fit very comfortably with the characteristics revealed as you consider your heritage. In this way, astronomy and archaeology come together to point the way forward.

The effective strategist and decision-maker can take inspiration from places such as Stonehenge, which have influenced the convergence of two seemingly separate disciplines into the study of 'Archaeoastronomy'. While it's well known that the stones line up with the points on the horizon where the sun rises on the summer solstice and sets on the winter solstice, further studies and excavations have revealed dozens more alignments with significant moments in the solar and lunar calendars.

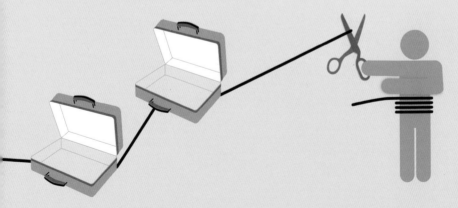

STRATEGIZI
ABOUT THE
RELATIONS
BETWEEN 1

NG IS

IPS
HINGS .

GEOGRAPHY

You have already looked upwards, to identify the 'North Star' direction and destination that really matter to you. You've dug down, so that you can act in alignment with your heritage, and not be tripped by your baggage. Now, before you reach your decision and set out on the journey of implementation, it's time to look around to assess the terrain; to look forward at the weather forecast; and to check your backpack to make sure you've got the right kit. The effective strategist is also a capable geographer.

In its definition of geography, the National Geographic Society emphasizes the dual focus, on places and on people. Some geographers might specialize in the former

(physical geography) or the latter (human geography), but the strategist is interested in the inter-relationship between the two.

'Geography is the study of places and the relationships between people and their environments. Geographers explore both the physical properties of Earth's surface and the human societies spread across it. They also examine how human culture interacts with the natural environment and the way that locations and places can have an impact on people. Geography seeks to understand where things are found, why they are there, and how they develop and change over time.'
National Geographic Society

In a digital age, satellite-enabled technologies mean that there are few places on the planet that remain unmapped, so you might think that 'terra incognita' is now a thing of the past. But in reality, constant changes are taking place in coastlines and watercourses, which mean that maps can't always keep up. Towns, cities and landscapes evolve, so using an old map can be risky. The same challenge applies when you make decisions. Social norms, markets and fashions change, as do people's preferences, and all sorts of other factors which might affect what you choose to do.

So it makes sense to formulate your own up-to-date map. As you do this, you can learn from those who sketched early geographical charts. At times when large parts of the world were unexplored, maps didn't just show travellers which way to go, they highlighted areas to be avoided, or at least where extra vigilance was advised, as well as useful points at which to replenish supplies, find fresh water or connect with friendly souls who might provide shelter. In a similar way, the strategist/decision-maker aims to identify and situate both the unhelpful and the helpful factors around them, so that they can choose the safest, speediest path to their desired outcome.

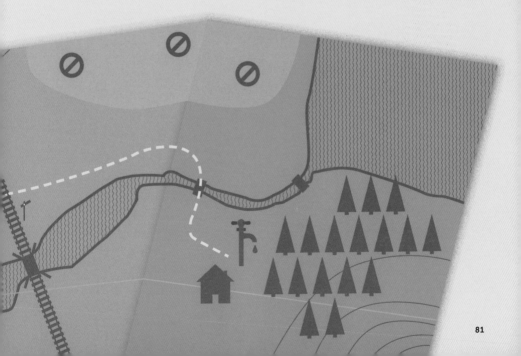

FROM SOFT TO SWOT

Imagine you're planning an epic road trip. There are several routes that you might take, based on how much time you have, the specific sights you want to see, and so on, but before choosing one you'll want to think about the vehicle in which you'll be travelling. How reliable is it? How many days' supplies can it comfortably hold? How far can it go before it needs recharging or refuelling?

Charting these two domains – the outer and the inner – onto a single map can be a rich source of strategic insight. In the 1960s, management consultant Albert Humphrey came up with a powerful framework to help with this, but it took him two attempts.

Leading a research project looking at corporate planning processes, Humphrey noticed that the factors considered important by the organizations he was studying could be divided into four categories: 'What is good in the present is Satisfactory, and what is good in the future is an Opportunity; What is

bad in the present is a Fault, and what is bad in the future is a Threat.'

Over time, it became clear that this SOFT analysis had its own significant fault, which limited its value as a planning tool: it made no distinction between factors that described the organization, and those that referred to the environment around the organization. This problem was solved when 'Satisfactory' became 'Strengths', and 'Faults' became 'Weaknesses', giving us one of those rare business models that has found its way into general use: the SWOT analysis.

SWOT's fame is deserved, not least because it manages to capture both the 'in here/out there' and the equally important 'now/future' dimension in such a simple formula. Some people say that it's really just a brainstorming tool, and too superficial to justify the title 'analysis', but from the perspective of the decision-making strategist, this criticism misses the point.

The legitimacy of SWOT doesn't necessarily depend on conducting an in-depth study. Much of the value is unlocked simply by asking the questions: 'What are my strengths and weaknesses in relation to this decision?' and 'What are the opportunities and threats out there?'

Once you've identified these, you can ask further questions to generate deeper insights.

- Which of my strengths equip me to exploit particular opportunities?
- Which of my weaknesses mean that I should be careful to avoid particular threats?
- What's the balance of opportunities and threats?
- Are any of the threats or weaknesses so influential that I need to address them separately before taking on the wider challenge?

'TAKING WHOLE'

A wealth of data may feel like a blessing or a curse. You want to cover all the angles, but you also want a coherent picture, pointing clearly to the best decision. Examining each piece of the jigsaw to work out where it fits may not be possible. The more effective route could be to look at all the pieces together. If you get this right, it could be equivalent to revealing the picture on the jigsaw puzzle box.

'Taking whole' is translated from a 2,500-year-old text, Sun Tzu's *The Art of War*. One of the book's central ideas is that every situation is imbued with different potential energies. Some will naturally tend towards your goal, while others will take you somewhere else. Determining which is which is not a purely intellectual process. It involves engaging your senses and getting to know the situation fully.

Sun Tzu calls the bridge from this broader, deeper form of knowing into decision-making and action: 'Shih'. He equates the use of this mysterious energy to 'rolling trees and rocks. When square, they stop. When round, they go.' The skilful general in Sun Tzu's book, or the better decision-maker in ours, knows when to nudge a 'round rock' in order to trigger a positive pattern of movement.

One way to explore Shih is to play Jenga, the game consisting of wooden blocks stacked in eighteen levels of three. The challenge is to take turns removing a brick from lower down the tower and adding it to the top. As the game progresses, this leaves gaps; the tower gets taller but less stable. The winner is the last player to add a block to the top before someone brings the whole thing crashing down.

For our purpose, it helps to switch the objective to simply building the tower as tall as possible. This makes it a collaborative effort, where the whole team either succeeds or fails. If some participants have played the game before, this frequently becomes a weakness, or baggage. Teams tend to look to them for up-front guidance: for example, deciding only to remove the middle bricks from the rows of three. Yet this is a hedgehog-style strategy (see Lesson 9), and unnecessarily limits the height that the tower can reach.

Successful Jenga players are foxes: they strategize rather than having a fixed strategy, and they do this by moving around the tower, poking the bricks – carefully – until they find one that *wants* to move. This involves being fully in the present, because every brick that moves creates or releases pressure elsewhere. A brick that was moveable before is now fixed, whereas one that was stuck becomes easy to pull out.

In Jenga, success comes from acting into the 'whole', and testing what's ready to go in the desired direction. Strategizing in a real-life situation can be exactly the same. When you've examined it from all angles, you can discover where the pressure points and workable elements are.

FORCE FIELD

Many decisions are an attempt to move from one situation (the current) to another (the desired future). By using the exercises in Lessons 9–11, we can identify factors that will help us get there (North Star/Strengths/Heritage), or hinder us (Weaknesses/Baggage/Threats).

But, as in Jenga, we may find that things are more fluid than that: making one move might free up what looked like a blockage, or create a new one. So, to see the whole as well as the parts, we need a framework that is more sophisticated and flexible than a simple 'balance sheet'. Enter 'Force Field Analysis'.

Its originator, Kurt Lewin, was a pioneer in the field of Group Dynamics. He didn't see things in black and white terms, but always looked for nuances and hidden currents. His insight was that the status quo, or current situation, is the result of a combination of forces, some of which might helpfully push it towards a desired future, but aspects of which will constrain it or even push it to a less advantageous position.

If the 'SWOT' could be seen as less than an analysis, the Force Field is more, as it doesn't just help you to describe a situation, it enables you to see it differently, and to change it.

The sequence of questions is important. Defining the desired future state first creates a North Star. Visiting the future first also means that, in considering Question 2, you can see the current situation with fresh eyes, and maybe spot something that you would have missed if you were only trying to 'escape the present'.

Questions 3 and 4 invite the decision-maker to see the elements influencing their situation not as static 'factors', but as dynamic 'forces', which can be harnessed or mitigated in order to move the status quo towards the desired future. The fact that Question 5 focuses on specific forces, rather than the whole, allows you to notice how, by addressing one part of the challenge or opportunity, you might free up the situation, or unintentionally create new blockers – just like Jenga!

FORCE FIELD ANALYSIS

1. What is the desired future situation?

3. What forces sit between the current situation and desired future, which could block progress and/or push things backward?

2. What is the current situation?

4. What forces sit behind the current situation, which could move things forward?

5. What actions can be taken to
mitigate / weaken the impact of specific forces in
(3) and harness /strengthen specific forces in (4)?

TOOLKIT

09

It's easier to make a good decision when you know where you're trying to go. Looking beyond our immediate impulses in order to identify our own 'North Star' could turn what looks like a challenging decision into an easy one.

10

Decisions will be more robust if they align with the history and characteristics of the person or people who will have to implement them. Knowing your heritage and baggage – both generally, and with regard to specific choices – will help you make decisions which are a good fit for you.

11

A clear examination of the external environment, combined with an honest appraisal of your own strengths and weaknesses, provides very helpful pointers on how to move forwards.

12

Organizing your data so that you can see both the parts and the whole, and examining it from all angles, gives you the best chance of influencing the situation in the way that you want.

FURTHER LEARNING

READ

The Rules of Victory: Strategies from The Art of War
James Gimian & Barry Boyce (Shambhala, 2008)

Theory U: Leading from the Future as it Emerges
C. Otto Scharmer (SoL, 2007)

The Hedgehog and the Fox: An Essay on Tolstoy's View of History
Isaiah Berlin (1953; W&N, 2014)

WATCH

How Great Leaders Inspire Action (Start with Why)
Simon Sinek, TED Talk

Fantastic Mr Fox
Directed by Wes Anderson, 2009

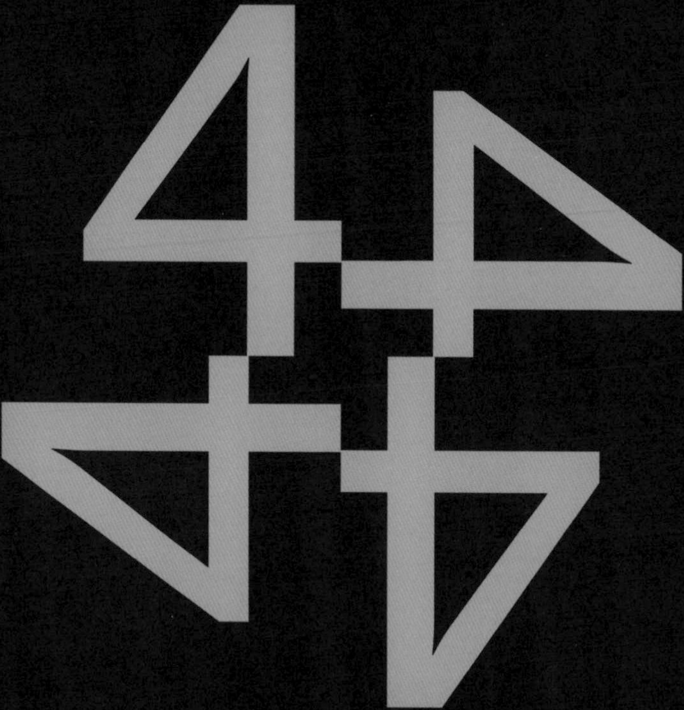

ALL TOGETHER NOW

LESSONS

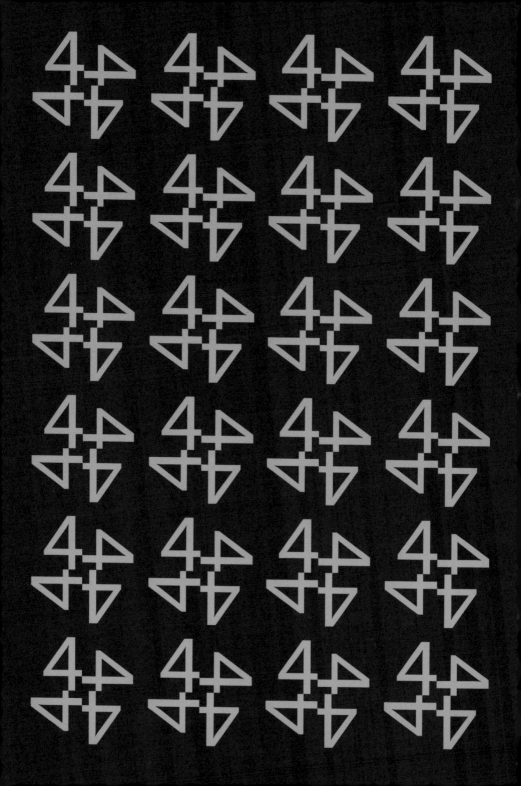

Before asking 'How can we make this decision together?', our first question is: 'Should we make this decision together?'

They say that two heads are better than one. When it comes to decision-making, is that always true? And if so, does the same logic extend to three heads? Eight? Eight hundred?

The answer depends on the distribution of two assets that hold the key to better decision-making: *wisdom* and *power*. Wisdom consists of knowledge, skill, awareness, or a combination of the three. Power is about who has the authority to make, or to influence, a decision.

Either one can be concentrated in an individual or spread across a group. When addressing the same decision, power and wisdom may be distributed in different ways. One person may have the power, but the wisdom may be shared across a team, a community or a whole population. Conversely, an individual may have the wisdom to make a decision, but need to bow to the authority of others.

Making better decisions in groups requires effort. Lesson 13 considers the reasons why this investment may be worthwhile, rather than deciding alone. Lesson 14 explains how decision-making power can move around within a group, and ways of managing this.

In Lesson 15, we'll look at what effective decision-making groups need, and the ways in which their capacity to make better decisions might be enhanced or diminished by the mysterious forces of group dynamics. Lesson 16 tackles the challenge of how to maximize the chances of a decision actually being implemented, once a group leaves the decision-making forum and reverts to being a collection of individuals.

Before asking 'How can we make this decision together?', our first question is 'Should we make this decision together?'

THE WISDOM OF GROUPS

If a broken-down car needs to be pushed to the side of the road, it's an advantage to have several helpers. Admittedly, beyond a certain number, it can become hard to co-ordinate their efforts. People whose preference is to make decisions by themselves might claim – with some justification – that involving others can be like having the pushers distributed around the four sides of a car. They'll cancel each other out, and probably get sweaty and frustrated in the process.

But, if a group is set up right, it can become a powerful decision-making machine. James Surowiecki demonstrates this in his book *The Wisdom of Crowds*, and

starts with an example from nineteenth-century rural England.

Following a visit to a country fair, the statistician Sir Francis Galton analyzed the 800 entries to a competition in which people guessed the weight of an ox. A believer in the superiority of the privileged few, Galton expected the ordinary folk who entered to be way off the mark. So he was surprised to find that the median guess was within 1 per cent of the actual weight of 1,198 pounds. Even more startling, a calculation of the mean average of all the guesses came up with the figure of 1,197, closer to the correct answer than any individual entry.

Galton concluded that his experiment pointed to 'the trustworthiness of a democratic judgement'. This phrase is a good summary of the rationale behind many markets and political systems, which trust 'the crowd' to make decisions. You may not have a crowd around you, but if others will be involved in implementing a decision, or even if they just have relevant knowledge or opinions, then it makes sense to involve them in making it.

There's an irony here, because Galton was also a leading figure in a movement embodying some of the most potent dangers associated with groups having the power to decide. These include 'group think', where an excessive desire to achieve consensus results in mistakes being made. In extreme cases, this can lead to 'mob rule'. Historically, the worst examples have often involved advocating the innate superiority of one group over others. Since World War 2, such beliefs have been discredited, and the person who gave them a veneer of scientific language, under the title 'Eugenics', has suffered severe damage to his reputation. That person was Sir Francis Galton. Yet, in considering whether to make a decision alone or to involve others, it's worth taking a closer look at some of the factors behind his country fair discovery.

ME OR WE?

James Surowiecki suggests that the effectiveness of the ox-weight competition entrants as a collective was based on three key factors.

The first was that everyone participating in the exercise was aiming to achieve one outcome – a correct answer to a clear question – and, having paid sixpence to enter, was motivated to give it their serious consideration. The second was that each person had made their own separate decision. It was only when these were aggregated that the 'wisdom of the crowd' emerged. Third, each participant had direct and equal access to the available data (in this case, simply being able to study the ox) and could make their own judgement.

Few situations in which we have the opportunity to make a decision alongside others will replicate these conditions fully. However, in judging whether or not to involve a broader group, they provide a very useful checklist:

☐ **01. To what extent do the group members have a shared understanding of what they're being asked to decide?**

☐ **02. To what extent are the group members motivated to give their best attention to the decision?**

☐ **03. Are individual group members likely to have – or to be able to develop – their own view?**

☐ **04. How accessible is the data that group members can draw on in making their decision?**

If the answers to any of these questions are negative, and you still want or need to involve the group, then correcting those factors before making the decision will save

you time and trouble, as well as improving the quality of the decision.

Even if the answers are positive, and you're confident that the group has sufficient wisdom, things could still be derailed by issues relating to power.

Imagine that eight participants at the country fair were randomly selected to work together as a 'jury' to come up with a single guess on behalf of the whole group. As soon as they assembled, hierarchies would emerge, which may or may not reflect any individual's ability to make a judgement, but would immediately affect who contributed to the conversation and how. In addition, the 792 who had not been selected might cast doubt on the qualifications of those who had, and attack their legitimacy in representing the whole group.

Political factors like these are as important in determining a group's decision-making effectiveness as their wisdom. So, two further questions can be added to our checklist:

05. Is the group recognized as having the authority to make a decision?

06. Will all group members feel able to make their full contribution, and allow others to do the same?

Ideally, we'd answer these questions *before* choosing whether to work as a group. However, the reality is that many group decisions happen in the context of established structures and systems, like families or management teams, where deciding together is the norm.

This doesn't mean that we leave behind our checklist of questions about wisdom and power. Quite the opposite: they may become even more important, in helping us make good choices about *how* we engage with the group in order to achieve the best possible result.

SHARING POWER

When working in a group, changing the way that power is distributed can lead to better decisions. This is true whether you're sitting around the boardroom table or the dinner table.

You might argue that our options about holding on to power, or sharing it out, are constrained by where we sit within an established hierarchy and how others see us. This is true, but it's important to remember that power and authority are not the same thing. Most organizations and societies are built around hierarchies designed to attach certain amounts of authority to specific roles. But just because someone has formal authority within a group, this doesn't mean that they can or should exercise the most power. Authority generally sits in a defined place, but power can flow in different directions.

The exercise below illustrates the dynamic, fluid nature of power.

+EXERCISE

Person 1 occupies a space – let's say a stage set designed to mirror a simple office – with a desk, chairs etc. Their task is to look as if they really own the place and are in charge.

Person 2 enters. Their brief is to immediately become the most powerful person in the scene. They might do this by striding confidently to the chair opposite Person 1 and putting their feet up on the desk.

In comes Person 3 with the same brief. They may carry this off by standing very close to Person 2, who is seated, towering over them and instructing them to take their feet off the desk. Each subsequent person has to become the most powerful character in the room, simultaneously removing power from the others and taking it for themselves.

Just as it's possible to take power, you can also share it, or give it to an individual or group. In contrast to the previous exercise, when power is shared, it becomes apparent that it's not a finite resource, where one person having more means that others automatically have less. An excellent leader can empower her team to make their own decisions and actually end up looking and being more powerful herself.

If you observe effective decision-making groups, you'll see that there is a clarity and comfort about who can contribute and how. Nothing may have been written down, but there's still a contract between the participants. Everyone has bought into the way that power is distributed and how it can move around the group. As you watch them, you're likely to find that, at any given moment, it sits in one of three places: with the group leader, with the group, or in-between the two.

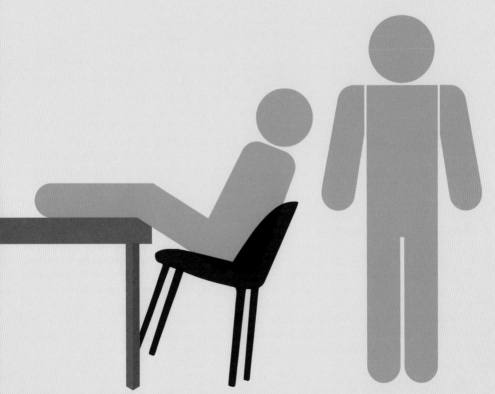

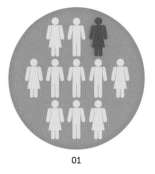

01   02   03

WHO'S IN CHARGE?

There are three basic power positions from which a group leader can operate:

01. It's Up To Me
The group leader makes choices on behalf of the group.

02. Let's Do This Together
The group leader makes choices with the group.

03. It's Up To You
The group decides.

'It's up to me' is the default setting for many group leaders. It's often an effective, efficient way of working, and groups generally value leaders who are willing to be decisive on their behalf. However, if the group will need to take ownership of decisions, and to work collaboratively or autonomously to deliver them, 'It's up to me' can put them in a passive frame of mind. Giving them opportunities to exercise their choice-making power by using 'Let's do this together' or 'It's up to

you' increases the chance of successful implementation and follow-through, once the decision has been made.

Of course, sharing power presents challenges. People might have different viewpoints, which could be hard to reconcile, or there may simply not be time to involve everyone.

Skilled group leaders recognize when these factors apply, but can still enable people to feel like active participants in the decision-making process, even when they're effectively being told what's going to happen. You can do this by separating the management of the content (*what* is discussed) from the process (*how* the encounter is organized). By mixing up the power dynamics, you can be directive (It's up to me) and inclusive (Let's do this together / It's up to you) at the same time.

Of the following interventions, only the first involves the group leader 'telling' the group what both the content and the process will be. The others all involve sharing some power.

	It's Up To Me	Let's Do This Together	It's Up To You
01. Before we move on, let's discuss X.	Content Process		
02. Based on our previous conversation, I've listed some possible talking points. Let's look through them and decide which to tackle.	Process	Content	
03. We need to devise action plans to achieve these three key objectives. We could break into smaller groups or stay together: which would work best?	Content	Process	
04. Please write down the two issues which are most important for us to consider. Then we'll cluster these and decide which to tackle first.	Process		Content
05. You've identified the areas where decisions are required. How do you want to handle these?			Content Process

You could argue that inviting the group to participate in choices about the process is not giving them real power. However, what matters here is not the focus of the choice, it's the group leader's level of sincerity – as perceived by the group – in the offer that they are making to allow the group to shape things. This can stimulate group members' pro-activity, even when the substance of a decision has already been determined. What a group feels is at least as important as what it thinks. This is why it helps to have some understanding of the mysterious world of group dynamics, and what a group needs.

WHEN IT C
DECISION -
ARE TWO H
BETTER TH

OMES TO
MAKING,
EADS
AN ONE?

WHAT GROUPS NEED

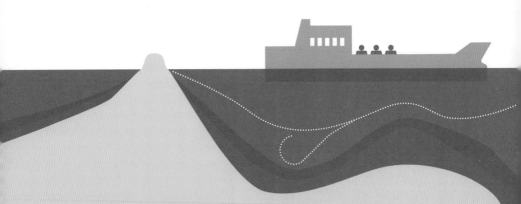

Operating in groups is essential not only to human development, but also to our survival. The world is a dangerous place, and some of those dangers can only be overcome by working together. But groups themselves can feel dangerous, and anxieties can be stirred up, which lead us to behave in ways that are not constructive.

The differences between a successful decision-making group and one that habitually makes mistakes or fails to reach a decision are often hard to identify. The same group can shift between being highly effective and seemingly dysfunctional – sometimes in the course of the same discussion. These movements are driven by group dynamics, which can be compared to the rocks, sandbanks or currents under the surface of the sea: they're frequently invisible, and they may sink you, if you don't know how to navigate through them.

In his 1961 work, 'Experiences in Groups',

Wilfred Bion mapped group dynamics with great clarity. Having commanded a tank in World War 1, and treated traumatized soldiers in World War 2, Bion had considerable experience of how groups operate under extreme pressure. His work as a psychoanalyst persuaded him that, even in more peaceful everyday situations, similar patterns could be observed. Examining these, he saw that certain dynamics arise in groups independently of what any individual might be thinking or feeling. These produce consistent patterns of behaviour, regardless of the cultural context or personality types.

Bion's defining insight is that, at a particular moment, any group is either focusing on its legitimate 'work' (i.e. making a decision) or it is unconsciously defending itself against anxiety. He described three observable patterns of behaviour, which indicate that a group is not in 'work' mode:

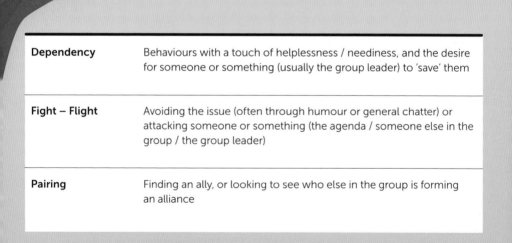

Dependency	Behaviours with a touch of helplessness / neediness, and the desire for someone or something (usually the group leader) to 'save' them
Fight — Flight	Avoiding the issue (often through humour or general chatter) or attacking someone or something (the agenda / someone else in the group / the group leader)
Pairing	Finding an ally, or looking to see who else in the group is forming an alliance

To be clear, these are not the insecurities, they are the responses to insecurity. They can be triggered by all kinds of feelings or events, some of which may have originated outside the group, but which individual group members have carried into it.

Learning to spot these signals, and to help groups overcome anxiety, could be key to effective decision-making. Along the way you'll probably encounter the choppy waters of group conflict, so you'll want to make sure you're properly protected.

THE VALUE OF CONFLICT

Having worked with thousands of groups, I've realized that the essential kit for anyone navigating their way through the rocks and currents of group dynamics is a wetsuit.

It's no accident that, in talking about group dynamics, weather and water metaphors keep cropping up. When things get tricky in a group, it can feel quite wild. One of the best-known theories about groups, Bruce Tuckman's 'Four Stages of Group Development', provides a great example. His central point is that, following on from the polite and tentative *forming* stage, there HAS to be conflict, or at least a clash of styles, opinions or personalities – *storming* – before the group can reliably agree its rules of engagement – *norming* – and get fully into work mode – *performing*.

Seeing conflict as a necessary step towards group effectiveness will help you respond to it calmly. It's important that you avoid getting drawn in. This is where the wetsuit comes in. You're not separate from the group, you're part of it, and therefore any feelings that are flowing around it will flow around you too. If you're not protected, you'll probably have similar responses to the rest of the group (dependency / fight-flight / pairing), which means that you won't be able to help them navigate the *storm* and reach *perform*. The answer is to be able to 'swim' in the group, but maintain a few millimetres' distance, in order to be able to see more clearly what will help them move forward.

So, when conflict does come up, rather than get anxious or embarrassed yourself, you might simply point out that it's there – 'Ah, so we disagree . . .' – and, in doing so, make it clear that this is a normal and helpful thing. Without this kind of intervention, hidden anxiety levels in the group might increase, moving them further away from being ready to work. Once the group realizes that it's ok to feel discomfort, and inevitable that people will have different views, they can move on.

The materials required to make a good group dynamics wetsuit are very similar to the approaches required to strategize effectively (see Chapter 3). When a group is experiencing anxiety, it can quickly lose sight of its objective (North Star), or bump into historical 'baggage'. Maintaining your own awareness of these helps you to keep things in perspective, and provides a protective barrier against being overwhelmed by the energy and emotion swirling around a group.

The group leader's role

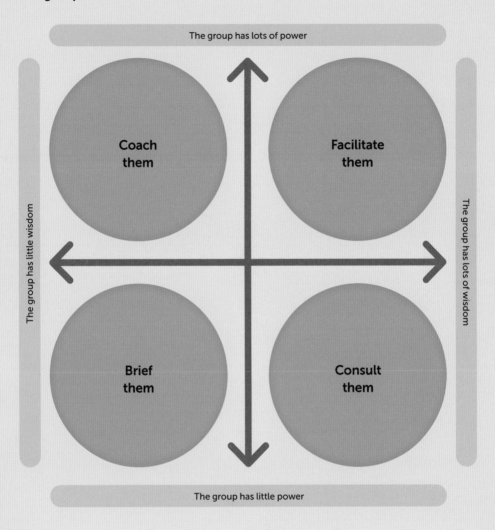

The group has lots of power

The group has little wisdom

The group has lots of wisdom

Coach them

Facilitate them

Brief them

Consult them

The group has little power

Perhaps the most important insight that you can gain while wearing your wetsuit is which leadership style or approach will be most helpful. A good way of assessing this relates to the group's levels of power and wisdom. If they've got lots of both, only minimal input will be required to facilitate them. If they have neither, you may need to brief them until you're confident that they understand what needs to be done. If they have lots of power or wisdom, but not both, coaching or consulting them could be the most helpful approach.

SEALING THE DEAL

A very important part of decision-making in groups is to provide a clear signal that a decision has been made. This could include a summary of what the decision is, but the most powerful message may be a symbolic one.

One of the most dramatic places to see decisions being made in public is at an auction. Although each individual is making their own judgements about whether and how much to bid, the group's collective actions will decide the ultimate price, and who will pay it.

A good auctioneer knows how to energize and engage the whole room. They speak animatedly, and aim to build momentum so that the value of bids goes up as quickly as possible. While an art or antiques auction might be very polite, an agricultural sale tends to be a louder affair. The participants will often be well acquainted with their rivals for the popular lots, so a degree of rowdiness is to be expected, and might even be encouraged.

Taken together, all of this is a recipe for confusion. But the auctioneer has a secret weapon: the wooden gavel (a hammer-shaped tool). It's usually held in such a way that the auctioneer can point the handle at the bidders as they name a price. And then,

when no more bids are forthcoming, they'll rap the gavel onto a hard surface, producing a sharp noise. The effect is both acoustic and symbolic. In that moment, there is no doubt that the bidding has ended and a conclusion has been reached. Like popping a balloon, the energy that has built up in the group dissipates, and the attendees are ready for the next item.

A good decision involves the bringing together of data, ideas and arguments into a unified, clear statement

A decision made by a group requires the various participants to converge onto a single viewpoint. Group members may have expressed different opinions during the debate, but at a certain moment there needs to be clarity that an agreed decision has been reached. It probably won't be appropriate to bang a gavel on a hard surface, but you can congratulate the group, or maybe just take a break before the next discussion item. This marks the boundary of the decision that has been made and shows the group members that the time for debate and consideration is over, and the time for clarity and action has arrived.

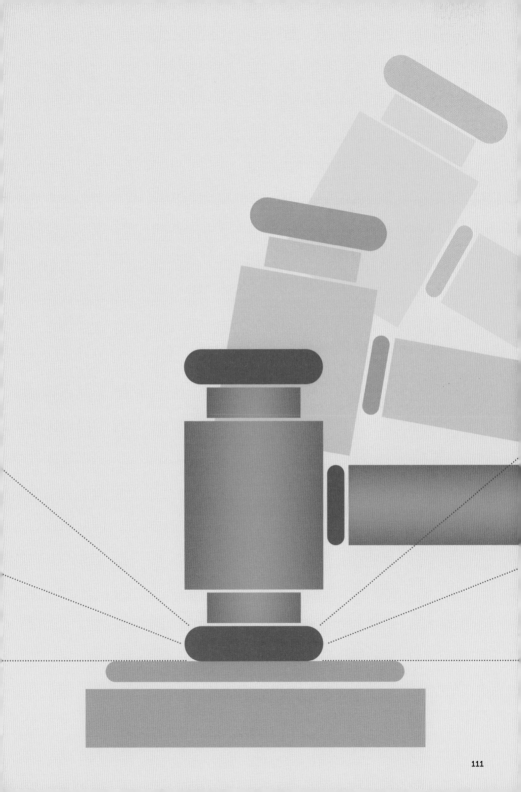

PHYSICAL CUES AND
BODY LANGUAGE

If the shape of a decision is < = > (see Chapter 2), then an important part of the group leader's role is to make it clear to the group which stage they're at. Just telling them isn't enough. People respond to energetic messages much more reliably than they do to the content of what is said. So how do you transmit the right messages? The most powerful way is through body language. And what's the most helpful body language? The decision-making shape provides some clues.

To bring this to life, let's imagine that our job is to guide a group, which could be family, colleagues or anyone else, through a decision-making process, and that the group is sitting around a table.

Sit by yourself at a table and imagine the group gathered around it. As you go through the stages, see if you can conjure the appropriate energy.

In the first stage, the Divergent, we sit upright and rest our arms on the table with our hands slightly further apart than our elbows, creating a version of the < shape, with our palms upwards. The energetic message to the group is 'I'm open; I'm inviting you to contribute; I'm pushing out the boundaries and wanting to hear more and more of what you have to say.'

In the second stage, the Emergent, we allow our body to come back a little, maybe supported by the back of the chair, but still alert and upright. We bring our elbows back and place our hands face-down on the table, with the fingers pointing straight ahead, so that our forearms and hands create a version of = . The energetic message to the group is: 'I'm still open, but there are now boundaries around the data that we've put on the table; let's play with that data and organize it and see what comes up.'

The third stage, the Convergent, looks and feels quite different to the group. We lean forward slightly, with our forearms on the table; our hands come together, with our fingers touching or interlocked. This creates the > shape. Once the decision is made, we sit up as tall as we can, with our arms and hands still in this shape > but the palms of our hands now forming a sharp point to the triangle. As we summarize the decision, we stay in this shape, and keep our sentences short, clear and authoritative. We're closing something down.

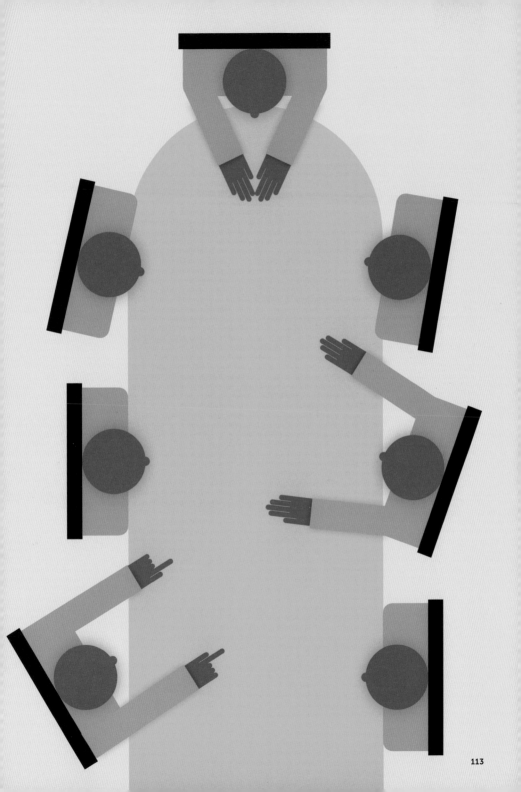

113

TOOLKIT

13

Groups can be powerful decision-making machines, but it helps if you make sure the members are engaged, well-informed, motivated, and have access to all the data they'll need.

14

Sometimes it's best to direct a group; on other occasions it's better to share power with them, or let them decide for themselves, especially if they'll need to engage actively in implementing the decision.

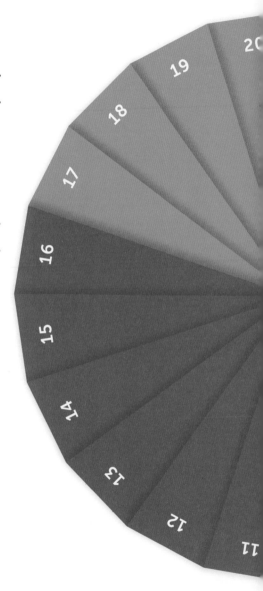

15

If a group is working to manage or overcome anxiety, it's not going to be able to focus on making a decision. Whatever your formal position, you may need to modify the role you play in order to help the group work constructively to reach a decision.

16

Groups respond more reliably to energetic and symbolic messages than verbal ones. If a decision has been reached, it's important to signal and reinforce this. Changing your body language can be a powerful tool in group decision-making.

FURTHER LEARNING

READ

The Wisdom of Crowds: Why the Many are Smarter Than the Few
James Surowiecki (Abacus, 2005)

The Complete Facilitator's Handbook
John Heron (Kogan Page, 1999)

Rebel Ideas
Matthew Syed (John Murray, 2019)

VISIT

Escape rooms provide a brilliant opportunity to experience and practise group decision-making – whether with your colleagues or with your family. Look out for one local to you and give it a try.

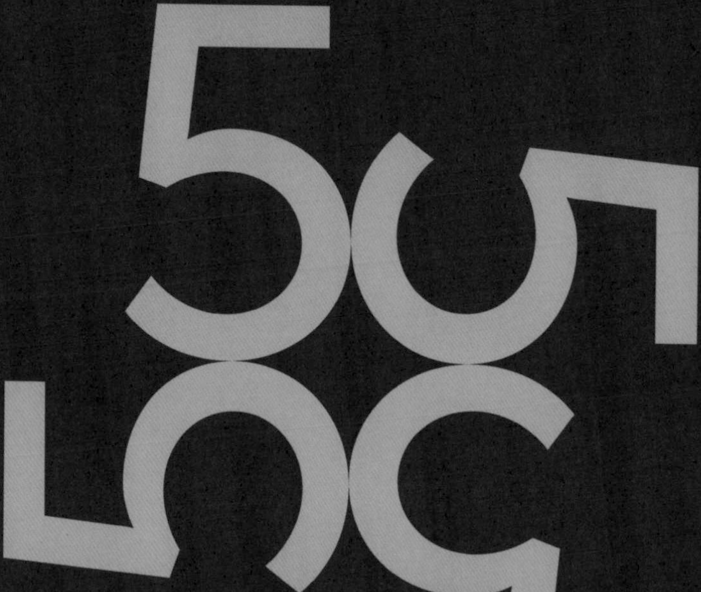

KNOW THYSELF

LESSONS

There is a lot to be said for looking in the mirror.

For more than a thousand years, those facing important decisions would travel great distances to the Temple of Apollo at Delphi. If they survived the rigours of the journey, they would face a series of interviews and tests before being granted an audience with the High Priestess, otherwise known as The Oracle. Demand for consultations was high: who wouldn't want guidance from the God of Truth, Healing and Prophecy? But the Oracle was only available one day each month, and most seekers never even got to ask their question.

To some, it may have come as a consolation that an all-purpose piece of wisdom was inscribed at the temple's entrance, and freely available to any visitor: 'γνῶθι σεαυτόν' ('KNOW THYSELF').

On the other hand, the inscription might have added to their frustration, with its suggestion that internal reference points are more important than advice from outside, even if you've crossed half an empire to get it.

Our starting point in this chapter is not to deny the value of advice from experts (or Gods, if you can access them), but to acknowledge that there is a lot to be said for looking in the mirror. The better you know your own motivations, habits and biases, the less likely you are to trip yourself up (Lesson 17). The more critically you're prepared to look at what you think you know, the more clearly you'll be able to see other points of view (Lesson 18). Cultivating your understanding of the environment that helps you to function at your highest level will enable you to create better conditions for your decision-making (Lesson 19). And being able to 'unhook' yourself from a fixed view of where you want to get to can open up new possibilities, and take the pressure out of even a high-stakes decision (Lesson 20).

LOOK IN THE MIRROR

I once attended a personal development workshop based on actors' training. The hardest exercise was the first night's 'homework', introduced as follows:

'The subject of this workshop is you. So your task between now and when we reconvene tomorrow is to study yourself . . . Literally! Find a quiet place and a mirror; set an alarm to five minutes, and stand in front of the mirror, looking at yourself.'

Hearing people's reports the next day, there was considerable diversity. Yet some patterns emerged. Everyone experienced five minutes as an eternity. Many were struck (pleasantly or otherwise) by their resemblance to parents or other family members. Once they got over their initial concerns about wrinkles and stray (or grey) hairs, some people were surprised by the feelings lurking in their expressions. What everyone agreed on was how novel it felt: most of us stand in front of a mirror every day, yet we hardly ever take a good, long look at ourselves.

In striving to be a better decision-maker, it pays to get a mirror out to examine our own biases and beliefs. We might like to think that our decisions are influenced solely by relevant facts. But if that is the case, why do different individuals, faced with similar data, often come up with different conclusions? The answers are to do with our distinct perceptions and interpretations of what's going on; with our deeper beliefs and attitudes; and with the lessons that we have absorbed – consciously or not – from our own experiences. The truth is that one of the biggest factors in any decision is likely to be Ourselves, yet it's one to which we generally pay little attention.

The challenge is that many valuable self-discoveries will not be sitting in plain sight. In order to access them, we'll have to get under the surface of our conscious minds and take a journey into our hidden depths.

Sigmund Freud, who pioneered the exploration of this mysterious territory, switched from using the word 'subconscious' to 'unconscious' in order to suggest that there is a clear, binary distinction between what we're conscious of and what we're not. Defined in this way, some of what sits in our unconscious will be things we used to know but have now forgotten. Alongside that, there may be aspects of our current situation, or data in front of us, that we can 'see', but that we haven't yet articulated to ourselves. As well as thoughts, feelings and information, there may be capabilities we're not even aware we have.

Any one of these elements may contribute to a better decision, so the task is to transfer as many of them as possible from the unconscious to the conscious realm.

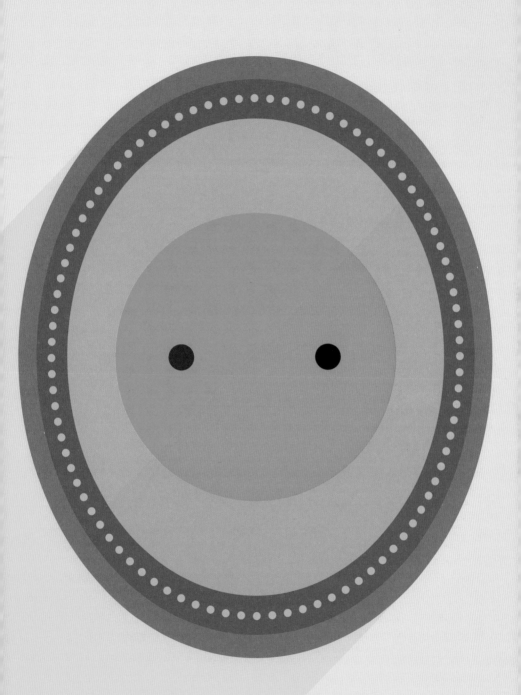

BENEATH THE SURFACE

Artists often work at the intersection of the conscious and unconscious mind. One of the great exponents of this was Salvador Dalí, who brought his unconscious into play by intentionally hovering between sleep and wakefulness. His technique was to sit in a chair with a key held between the thumb and forefinger of one hand, and a plate on the floor beneath it. He would relax and slip into slumber, at which point the key would fall onto the plate and wake him up. He would then capture the images playing in his mind at that moment in a sketchbook.

Less elaborate, and perhaps more reliable, is 'free-writing'. In her book, *The Artist's Way*, originally designed as a course for artists whose creativity was blocked, Julia Cameron suggests that as soon as possible after waking in the morning you should simply write whatever comes to mind onto three pages of a handily placed notebook; the objective is to get it onto the page as fast as your hand can move, and not to worry about whether the content makes any sense, whether it's grammatically correct, or even if it's particularly legible. The idea of these 'morning pages' is not to generate ideas (although that may well happen), but to bring to the surface all those thoughts and feelings – negative and positive; important and trivial – that are taking up space in the mind.

The effect of doing the 'morning pages' every day for a couple of weeks is a bit like studying yourself in the mirror. After a while, you start noticing recurring themes or surprising anomalies in what you've written: a seemingly minor task might be nagging at you; a setback you thought you were over may still be causing you pain; or there may be an ambition or desire locked up within you that you need to acknowledge and fulfil.

Of most value to the decision-maker, though, are the signs that point to your opinions and preferences: what attracts you and what turns you off? What are you afraid of? What's important to you? These elements may or may not point you to your decision, but if they remain below the surface, they could be distorting your perception of what's going on and your judgement about what to do. Once they're surfaced, you can factor them into your decision-making.

You can use the free-writing technique to address a specific decision. Set yourself a target (i.e. to fill three pages as quickly as possible), identify a defining question, and simply write whatever comes into your head – even if it's gobbledegook. When you've finished, put the pages to one side for a few minutes before you read them, then treat the exercise as if you are prospecting for nuggets or clues rather than expecting a fully formed answer. In this way you may capture relevant ideas, knowledge or awareness that have been sitting in your unconscious mind. The most useful material often appears at the end, so keep going!

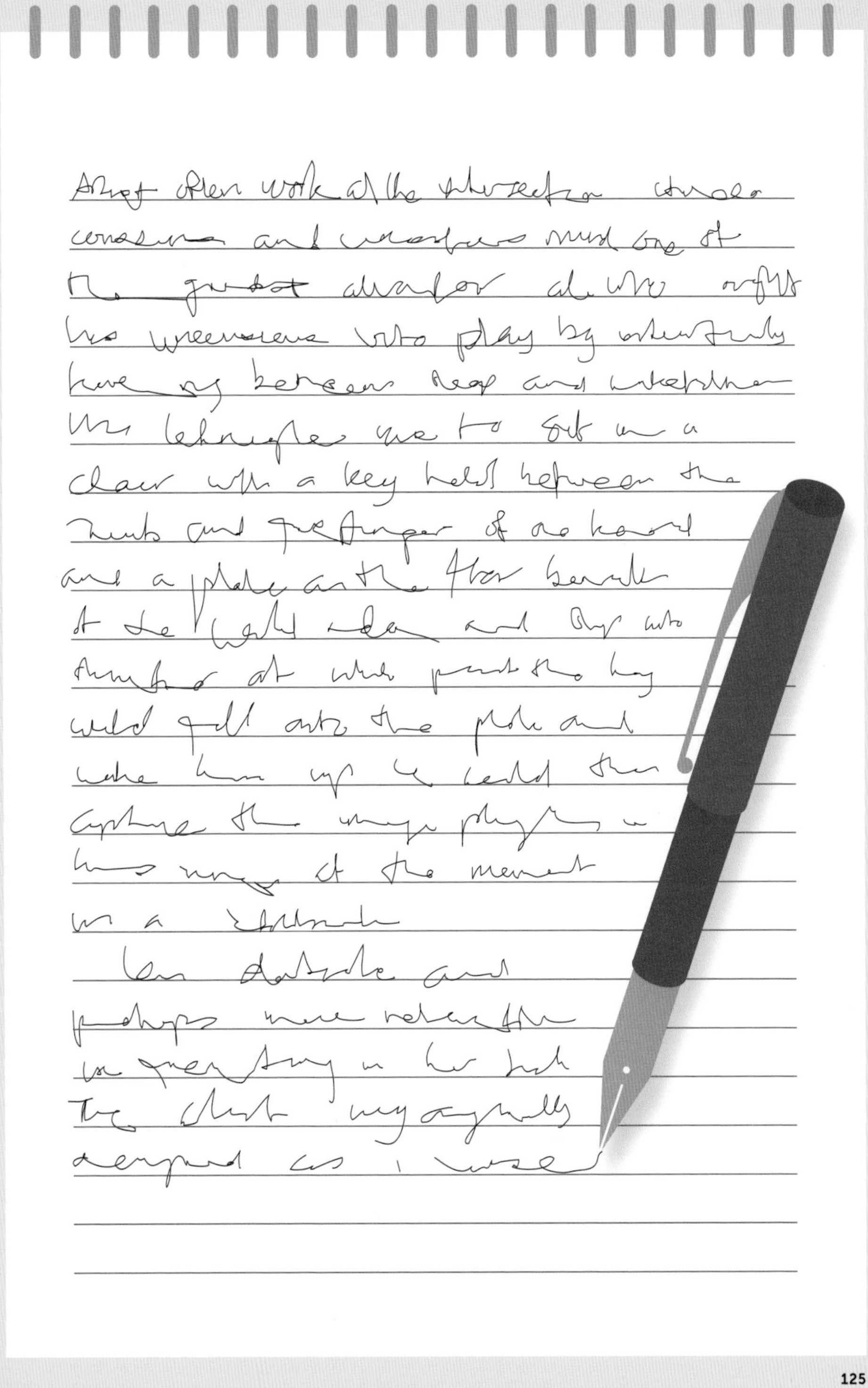

18
BUILD +
BECOME

THE VALUE OF IGNORANCE

Scientists are associated with knowledge, yet in reality they should be seen as experts in *not knowing*: much of a scientist's work addresses questions to which they don't know the answer . . . yet. Similarly, the greatest chunk of the decision-maker's time is spent in the space before a decision has been made. As a consequence, we need to build our tolerance to not knowing, and to understand our own relationship with what we know, or believe we know.

A few years ago, I was working on a series of workshops with groups drawn from the arts and from banking. All the managers on the programmes had similar levels of responsibility in their different organizations.

At a certain point, I introduced an exercise designed to help the participants examine and develop their relationship with knowing and not knowing. Knowing – and showing it – can build confidence, clarity and direction. Not knowing leaves room for discovery, and, from a leadership viewpoint, makes space for team members to step up and take responsibility.

The exercise involved each individual repeating 'I know' and 'I don't know' as they moved around, and then discussing the different feelings and atmospheres generated in the room by the two phrases. The pattern for most people is that 'I know' comes more easily, and creates a positive feeling; when they get to 'I don't know', energy levels go down, and many people avoid eye contact or feel some discomfort. There are, however, usually some individuals for whom the opposite applies: they don't enjoy 'I know', and are relieved and energized when they're allowed to say 'I don't know'.

On this occasion, almost all the leaders from the arts felt more comfortable with 'I don't know'. When we discussed why this might be, they reflected that, when working with artists to stage exhibitions or put on productions, flexibility and creativity are generally more important than certainty.

Undertaking the same exercise, the bankers were happy with 'I know', but when invited to switch to 'I don't know', they rebelled. At first, they could not accept that there were circumstances in which an 'I don't know' approach could be desirable. This is understandable. From early childhood, there aren't many occasions on which you're rewarded for letting others see that you don't know. And in the environment of their bank, the participants felt that this would invite disrespect, or even punishment.

The irony is that these workshops took place just a few months after the 2008 financial crash, and before there had been a thorough examination of its causes. When that eventually happened, one of the most powerful findings was that banking executives had been dealing with products and concepts that most of them didn't understand, but none of them dared admit it. Their attachment to 'I know' was such that they never asked the questions that might have revealed the extent of the risks to which they were exposing their businesses and the wider economy.

126

MAYBE

Even if, like the artists, you're comfortable with not knowing, making a decision still requires you to travel from 'I don't know' to 'I know', and the safest path is via 'maybe' (below).

Scientists understand this, which is why one of their key tools is the hypothesis, used as a bridge from what is known now to what might be proved in the future.

Being willing to adopt a hypothetical 'maybe' approach gives us the opportunity to explore multiple potential futures before making a firm decision. Smart planners in government, community development, business and the military devise scenarios:

stories about different versions of the future. This could be seen as arrogance, but the accusation would only stick if there was just one story. By coming up with three or four possibilities, this approach acknowledges that nobody can know the future.

More informally, when someone asks: 'What's the best thing that could happen?', they're inviting you to adopt a scenario-like approach. When they ask 'What's the worst thing that could happen?', they're reflecting the fact that even very important decisions rarely lead to a life-or-death outcome. In fact, the consequences of decisions

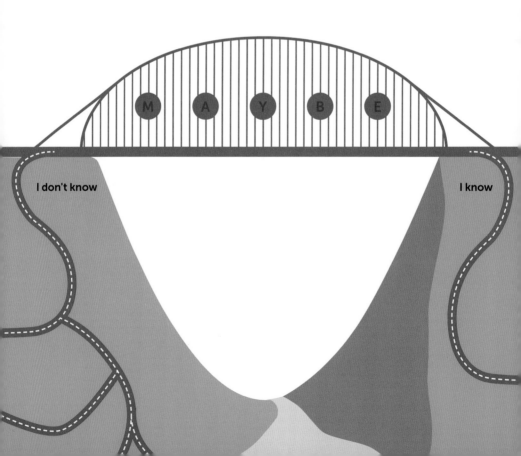

are usually a combination of positive and negative.

'Maybe' can cover a broad range, from almost no chance to almost certain. So it helps if you can map different options to see where they sit. If you combine this with the fact that most decisions will have a mixture of positive and negative consequences, you can plot them onto this matrix (below).

Try it: take one of your three test-case decisions, and identify two possible answers. Now, using a different coloured pen or pencil for each one, see if you can identify at least one potential consequence in each box. Depending on the nature of the decision, you may end up choosing to go with the option which carries fewer 'Highly Probable' / 'Worst Case' consequences, even if it has an attractive 'Best Case'.

Either way, undertaking this exercise provides the opportunity to take a stroll into possible futures.

It also means that, by the time you implement your decision, you've already thought about what signals to look out for, in order to assess whether it's working or whether some adjustment or revision is required.

In using 'maybe' methodologies, the wise decision-maker will assume that very little that she writes down will come to life exactly in the way that is anticipated. To acknowledge this is a strength, because it reflects the reality that it's impossible to know what's going to happen. The making of a decision is generally just the starting point for a process of close observation of what happens, in preparation for the next decision to be made.

Example: I feel undervalued at work. What shall I do?

Decision (01) Ask my boss for a pay rise
Decision (02) Keep my head down and hope someone will notice

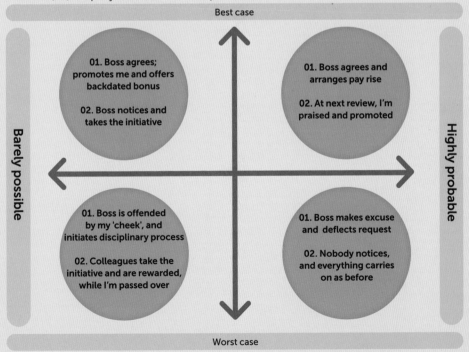

Best case

01. Boss agrees; promotes me and offers backdated bonus

02. Boss notices and takes the initiative

01. Boss agrees and arranges pay rise

02. At next review, I'm praised and promoted

Barely possible — Highly probable

01. Boss is offended by my 'cheek', and initiates disciplinary process

02. Colleagues take the initiative and are rewarded, while I'm passed over

01. Boss makes excuse and deflects request

02. Nobody notices, and everything carries on as before

Worst case

IT PAYS TO
OUR OWN B
BELIEFS.

EXAMINE
ASES AND

THERE'S A PLACE FOR US

When a friend or colleague is facing a major life-changing fork in the road, it can be hard to know how to help them. Even if we have a view about what they should do, it is clear that this has to be their own decision. When the stakes are very high, it's wise to ask ourselves if we're ready to take responsibility for the consequences of our advice. Even if we try to avoid telling them what to do, by asking a question or talking in generalities ('Follow your heart'), we may trigger an unhelpful reaction or interrupt their thought process.

And yet we still want to offer real, tangible help, and not just go through the motions.

A reliable way of doing this, while avoiding the many pitfalls of offering advice, is to focus not on the question to be resolved, but on the environment that will be most helpful for them. By asking: 'Where's a good place for you to make this decision?', we're giving our friend or colleague an opportunity to look in the mirror and think about what helps them to operate at their highest level. By reminding them that they have a choice, we're empowering them. In considering their answer to our question, they're likely to think about the sources of information and support that they'll need, and how to access them.

What's striking, in my experience of asking this question, is that people generally don't find it difficult to come up with an answer. With regard to big decisions, they instinctively know a good place to go.

The question may actually be harder to answer when the decision to be made is more routine. It can also be difficult when other people need to be involved. But the question is still worth asking, and it may lead a management team to organize their meeting off-site, or a married couple to wait until the weekend when they can take a walk together in the park, to make their decision.

The effectiveness of the 'walk in the park' is not just about the environment. In a one-on-one walk and talk, the fact that there can be comfortable pauses, which would be awkward if you were facing each other, and that you are in motion together, improves the quality of listening and shared reflection.

WHERE TO DECIDE?

As human beings, we are influenced by what's around us. Retailers manipulate the decor and layout of their shops to get us to buy more; prison administrators organize cells and communal areas in order to minimize trouble; trading floors, classrooms and factories are designed to enable particular tasks to be carried out effectively.

If asked to create the perfect decision-making environment, designers would look at variables such as lighting sources (natural daylight helps); noise levels (a slight background buzz beats both silence and high volume); colour schemes (yellow brings out your creativity, green calms you down); or even ceiling height (higher for more abstract or strategic decisions; lower for more concrete, immediate ones).

I imagine that you don't have the time or inclination to get out a paintbrush, let alone make structural alterations to your workspace, your kitchen or wherever you might be making your decisions. But you probably do have some freedom to move, and finding a place which suits you could make a real difference.

So what is the best environment in which to make better decisions? Well, that depends on the decision, but also on you. Maybe you're a go-for-a-walk kind of person; maybe you need a shot of adrenaline and the feeling of serious pressure before you can get to the heart of the matter; perhaps you need to sleep on it, or go to the gym, or the theatre, and forget all about it for an hour or two.

All of these are legitimate approaches, and as with many of the techniques in this book, you'll often find that simply asking the question 'Where do I need to be to help me make this decision?' will bring up ideas and energies which will tell you what you need to do.

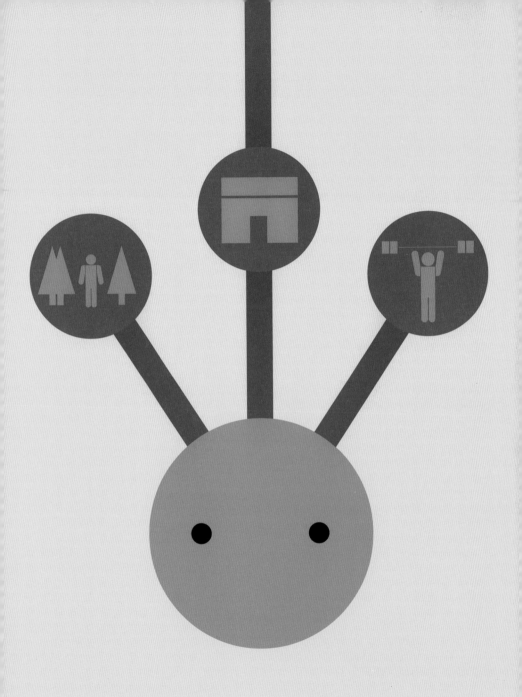

DETACH YOURSELF

If you've studied this book in the hope that you'll be able to eliminate risk or uncertainty from your decision-making, you're probably feeling disappointed right now. Nobody can know the future. Factors that seemed unrelated to your decision can turn out to be pivotal. People, organizations, markets, families and nature can all act in unpredictable ways.

In general, humans have one of two responses when we come face to face with the inescapable unknowability of the future: meek acceptance that our destiny is not in our own hands, or an impulse to fight to take control. These may look like opposites, but the reality is that, in both cases, we're allowing an unknown future to set our agenda: we're hooked!

The answer is to adopt an attitude that doesn't just contribute to better decision-making, but increases your happiness, and maybe even prolongs your life. These are big claims, but they're backed up by a practice that has been a recurring feature in religious and philosophical traditions for thousands of years: non-attachment.

One of the best ways to understand non-attachment is to consider its opposite. Attachment is a powerful driver of much human behaviour, and the source of immense quantities of frustration, conflict and stress. It consists of holding on to a particular view of a thing, a relationship, a person or an idea as being right or desirable.

When attachment is focused on something we've already got, we try to 'freeze' that thing; to retain it in its current form. But nothing lasts for ever, and everything changes, so this is doomed to failure. When attachment is applied to something we don't yet have, it stirs up anticipation of what it will feel like to have that thing. Even if we ultimately get what we thought we wanted, the chances are that the actual experience won't match our expectation. In both cases, we're setting ourselves up for disappointment.

Non-attachment is not an argument in favour of giving up. You can still have a burning aspiration, take a bold decision and act on it wholeheartedly. The difference is that, once you've acted, rather than holding on to a particular view of what you would like the result to be, you become curious and observe what actually happens next. This enables you to come more fully into the present moment rather than trying to hold on to something from the past, or to grasp for something in the future. In this way, it can actually help you to be more resolute and focused in your decisions and actions.

YOUR DECISION-MAKING EQUIPMENT

As you've read this book, you've probably found yourself responding not only in different ways (that's helpful / unhelpful / intriguing) but also from different places within yourself: head (that does / doesn't make sense); heart (I like that); and gut (that doesn't feel right).

The same three parts of our anatomy come into play when we're making decisions. These references might sound like metaphors, but they're actually quite literal: there are more neurons (the basic building blocks of the brain) located in the human gut area than most mammals have in their actual brains.

If there's a conflict between what we think (head); what we feel (heart); and what we intuit (gut), it could be confusing to have these different aspects of ourselves conducting an inner argument. However, the better decision-maker understands that it's a bonus to be able to process data through these filters. It's like having three different apps or software packages that we can use individually or in tandem.

To access their full benefits, we need to become familiar with the OS (operating system) that enables us to recognize which aspect of our intelligence is dominant in any particular moment and to switch between them. That OS is the autonomic nervous system, which runs our basic bodily functions, such as breathing and heartbeat. It has two basic modes: the sympathetic and the parasympathetic. Because the energy and rhythms that each bring are so different, they will profoundly affect the kind of decision that we are likely to make.

The sympathetic is often referred to as our 'accelerator'. When triggered – for example by something that we find threatening or exciting – our heart rate and breathing will speed up, adrenaline will wash through our bodies, and the oldest part of our brain, the 'reptilian', which drives our most basic impulses, will take over.

The parasympathetic is our 'brake'. When it's engaged, we're able to broaden our perspective and engage the prefrontal cortex, which is the area of our brain governing judgement, planning and motivation.

The key to better decision-making is often simply to be able to access the brake. Yes, the accelerator can be helpful if our back is genuinely against the wall, and an instant response is required, but when someone takes a long breath before making a difficult choice, what they're doing – quite naturally – is engaging their more spacious parasympathetic state and bringing their more sophisticated capabilities into play.

Wendy Palmer has combined knowledge from neuroscience, mindfulness and Aikido to develop a 'centering technique', which anyone can use to access their parasympathetic system. The first step is to take a deep breath, and let it out in a long exhale. Just doing this will shift your energy and engage your better decision-making capabilities. The full technique – and the science behind it – is set out in the book *Leadership Embodiment*, written with neuroscientist Janet Crawford.

Let's use the first part of Wendy's centering technique to identify the most important lessons that you can take from this book.

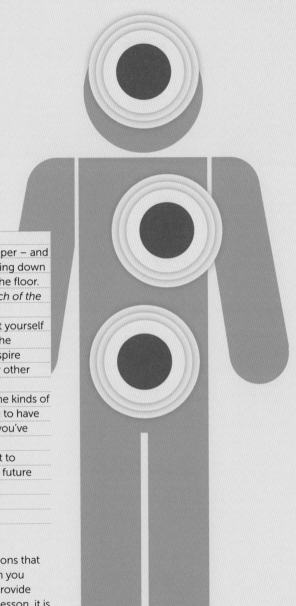

+EXERCISE

01. Take a deep breath.

02. Take another breath – even deeper – and this time imagine yourself exhaling down slowly through your body into the floor. (*Repeat this breath between each of the following stages.*)

03. Ask yourself how you *feel* about yourself as a decision-maker. Which of the elements that we've covered inspire excitement, nervousness or any other emotion?

04. What's your gut feeling about the kinds of situations in which you're going to have opportunities to practise what you've learned?

05. What do you think it's important to remember when you're making future decisions?

Do you remember those real decisions that you identified in Lesson 1, for which you were hoping that this book might provide some guidance? As this is the final lesson, it is a good moment to review any ways in which the ideas and techniques that we've explored might shape your actual decisions.

TOOLKIT

17

Self-awareness is very important in effective decision-making. Using techniques that surface your own hidden thoughts and feelings can prevent you from falling into self-deception or the repetition of old habits and reveal clues about what your decision needs to be.

18

Being comfortable with not knowing can open the door to new ideas, or to a more balanced insight into the data that you have. Rather than leaping from not knowing to a firm conclusion, it's useful to try out different hypotheses and see which one works best.

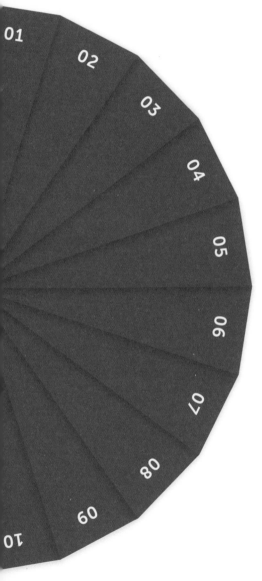

19

The location or environment within which you make a decision can have a positive or negative impact. Before trying to make a challenging decision, it can be helpful to think about the best place to go in order to make it.

20

If you hold on tight to a specific outcome, you're probably setting yourself up for disappointment. Relaxing and letting go doesn't mean that you don't care – instead, it can enable you to access your emotional and intuitive intelligence alongside your rational mind.

FURTHER LEARNING

READ

The Big Short
Michael Lewis (Penguin, 2011)

Comfortable With Uncertainty
Pema Chödrön (Shambhala, 2018)

Obliquity: Why our Goals are Best Achieved Indirectly
John Kay (Profile, 2011)

Leadership Embodiment: How the Way We Sit and Stand Can Change the Way We Think and Speak
Wendy Palmer & Janet Crawford (2013)

TRY

Wendy Palmer has combined knowledge from neuroscience, mindfulness and Aikido to develop a technique to boost the parasympathetic nervous system, shift your energy and engage your better decision-making capabilities.
www.leadershipembodiment.com

TRAIN

The Mastery
www.themastery.com
An acting-based workshop encouraging personal development and self-discovery.

WATCH

The Language of the Unknown: A Film about the Wayne Shorter Quartet
Directed by Guido Lukoschek, 2013

How Architecture Helped Music Evolve
David Byrne, TED Talk

EPILOGUE

Making a decision, then making another, and another . . . is central to the way in which humans live and learn. If you watch a toddler absorbed in the challenge of fitting the correct block into the star-, circle-, square- or triangular-shaped holes in a board, you'll see her trying one thing and then the next. This is experiential learning, and its importance extends into adulthood. It requires us first to act, then to review our action and its effects before planning what to do next.

The many teams and organizations around the world that have adopted the principles developed in Japan under the title 'Kaizen' – continuous improvement – are basically committed to the same cycle: Plan (identify your challenge); Test (try out possible solutions); Check (study the results); Act (implement the best solution); Plan Again (identify your next challenge) . . . and so on.

This perspective matters a great deal,

because it can take some of the pressure out of your decision-making. It's true that some decisions are definitive: once made, they set a course from which no deviation or backtracking will be possible. However, such forks in the road come along quite rarely. Life is essentially emergent. Something can be decided, or even seemingly concluded, then something else will happen and further decisions will need to be made.

A central message of this book is that it's often better to defer taking a decision (making a choice) until you've made the decision (given it proper consideration). But it's also important to acknowledge that sometimes you just need to get on with things; to make your choice and see what happens, in the knowledge that you'll have further opportunities to decide.

In a group situation, diving into making decisions together and following through on them might not just be the most effective

Sometimes you just need to get on with things; to make your choice and see what happens.

way to build trust and enhance performance, it might be the only way.

Our individual decisions shape our lives, and our collective decisions shape the world. That's why it's worth investing serious thought in how we approach and undertake them. But my final suggestion to you picks up on something else that we can learn from that toddler, busy fitting shapes into her board. For as long as it holds her interest, she takes the task seriously. But she doesn't take herself too seriously. This

is a classic trap, which extends beyond an exaggerated sense of self-importance into excessive reliance on particular frameworks, theories and approaches. There are many defences against falling into it, including curiosity and humility. Learning more directly from our two-year-old role model, one of the most powerful and effective antidotes is the maintenance of a healthy sense of playfulness.

Hopefully, you've had some fun playing with the ideas and exercises in this book, many of which I've visited and revisited over the years, and which have evolved in ways that continue to shed more light on my own decision-making and my reading of the world around me. I hope that at least some of them will serve you in the same way, and that you'll not only be able to apply what you've learned, but adapt the tools and techniques to suit you as you set about making your own better decisions.

BUILD + BECOME

At BUILD+BECOME we believe in building knowledge that helps you navigate your world.

Our books help you make sense of the changing world around you by taking you from concept to real-life application through 20 accessible lessons designed to make you think. Create your library of knowledge.

BUILD + BECOME
www.buildbecome.com
buildbecome@quarto.com

@buildbecome
@QuartoExplores

Using a unique, visual approach, Gerald Lynch explains the most important tech developments of the modern world – examining their impact on society and how, ultimately, we can use technology to achieve our full potential.

From the driverless transport systems hitting our roads to the nanobots and artificial intelligence pushing human capabilities to their limits, in 20 dip-in lessons this book introduces the most exciting and important technological concepts of our age, helping you to better understand the world around you today, tomorrow and in the decades to come.

Gerald Lynch is a technology and science journalist, and is currently Senior Editor of technology website TechRadar. Previously Editor of websites Gizmodo UK and Tech Digest, he has also written for publications such as *Kotaku* and *Lifehacker*, and is a regular technology pundit for the BBC. Gerald was on the judging panel for the James Dyson Award. He lives with his wife in London.

GERALD LYNCH

BUILD + BECOME

GET TECHNOLOGY

BE IN THE KNOW.
UPGRADE YOUR FUTURE.

KNOW TECHNOLOGY TODAY, TO EQUIP YOURSELF FOR TOMORROW.

Using a unique, visual approach to explore philosophical concepts, Adam Ferner shows how philosophy is one of our best tools for responding to the challenges of the modern world.

From philosophical 'people skills' to ethical and moral questions about our lifestyle choices, philosophy teaches us to ask the right questions, even if it doesn't necessarily hold all the answers. With 20 dip-in lessons from history's great philosophers alongside today's most pioneering thinkers, this book will guide you to think deeply and differently.

Adam Ferner has worked in academic philosophy both in France and the UK, but much prefers working outside the academy in youth centres and other alternative learning spaces. He is the author of *Organisms and Personal Identity* (2016) and has published widely in philosophical and popular journals. He is an associate editor of the Forum's *Essays*, and a member of Changelings, a North London fiction collaboration.

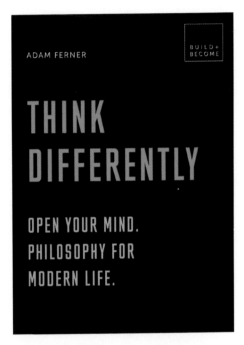

ADAM FERNER

BUILD+
BECOME

THINK DIFFERENTLY

OPEN YOUR MIND.
PHILOSOPHY FOR
MODERN LIFE.

PHILOSOPHY IS ABOUT
OUR LIVES AND HOW WE
LIVE THEM.

Using a unique, visual approach to explore the science of behaviour, *Read People* shows how understanding why people act in certain ways will make you more adept at communicating, more persuasive and a better judge of the motivations of others.

The increasing speed of communication in the modern world makes it more important than ever to understand the subtle behaviours behind everyday interactions. In 20 dip-in lessons, Rita Carter translates the signs that reveal a person's true feelings and intentions and exposes how these signals drive relationships, crowds and even society's behaviour. Learn the influencing tools used by leaders and recognize the fundamental patterns of behaviour that shape how we act and how we communicate.

Rita Carter is an award-winning medical and science writer, lecturer and broadcaster who specializes in the human brain: what it does, how it does it, and why. She is the author of *Mapping the Mind* and has hosted a series of science lectures for public audience. Rita lives in the UK.

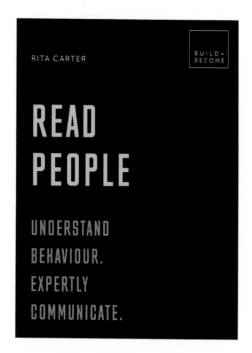

Disagreements are a fact of life. Productive disagreements are a rarity. We find ourselves living in a divided world in which it's increasingly difficult to have productive arguments.

In 20 thought-provoking discussions, philosophers Adam Ferner and Darren Chetty examine some of today's most pressing debates in politics, society and education. Opening up conversations about conversation, they offer helpful ways to navigate personal and political conflicts.

Adam Ferner has worked in academic philosophy both in France and the UK, but much prefers working outside the academy in youth centres and other alternative learning spaces. He has written two books, *Organisms and Personal Identity* (2016) and *Think Differently* (2018), and has published widely in philosophical and popular journals. He is an associate editor of the Forum's *Essays*, and a member of the Changelings, a North London fiction collaboration.

Darren Chetty has published academic work on philosophy, education, racism, children's literature and hip-hop culture. He is a contributor to the bestselling book, *The Good Immigrant*, co-author of *What Is Masculinity? Why Does It Matter? And Other Big Questions* and co-editor of *Critical Philosophy of Race and Education*.

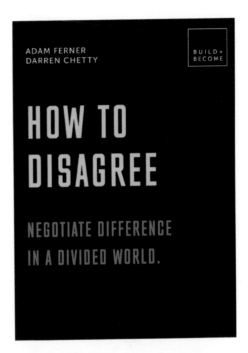

ADAM FERNER
DARREN CHETTY

BUILD +
BECOME

HOW TO DISAGREE

NEGOTIATE DIFFERENCE IN A DIVIDED WORLD.

HOW CAN WE DISAGREE PRODUCTIVELY?

Through a series of 20 practical and effective exercises, all using a unique visual approach, Michael Atavar challenges you to open your mind, shift your perspective and ignite your creativity. Whatever your passion, craft or aims, this book will expertly guide you from bright idea, through the tricky stages of development, to making your concepts a reality.

We often treat creativity as if it was something separate from us – in fact it is, as this book demonstrates, incredibly simple: creativity is nothing other than the very core of 'you'.

Michael Atavar is an artist and author. He has written four books on creativity – *How to Be an Artist, 12 Rules of Creativity, Everyone Is Creative* and *How to Have Creative Ideas in 24 Steps – Better Magic*. He also designed (with Miles Hanson) a set of creative cards '*210CARDS*'.

He works 1-2-1, runs workshops and gives talks about the impact of creativity on individuals and organizations. www.creativepractice.com

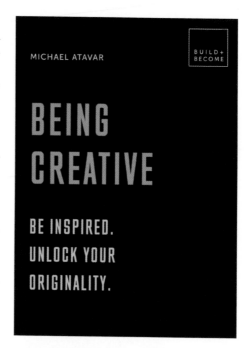

CREATIVITY BEGINS WITH YOU.

We are living longer than ever and, thanks to technology, we are able to accomplish so much more. So why do we feel time poor? In 20 eye-opening lessons, Catherine Blyth combines cutting-edge science and psychology to show why time runs away from you, then provides the tools to get it back.

Learn why the clock speeds up just when you wish it would go slow, how your tempo can be manipulated and why we all misuse and miscalculate time. But you can beat the time thieves. Reset your body clock, refurbish your routine, harness momentum and slow down. Not only will time be more enjoyable, but you really will get more done.

Catherine Blyth is a writer, editor and broadcaster. Her books, including *The Art of Conversation* and *On Time*, have been published all over the world. She writes for publications including the *Daily Telegraph, Daily Mail* and *Observer* and presented *Does Happiness Write White?* for Radio 4. She lives in Oxford.

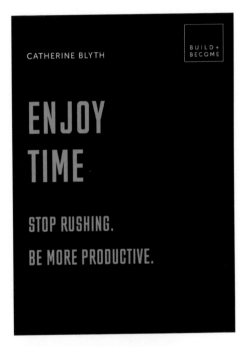

CATHERINE BLYTH

BUILD + BECOME

ENJOY TIME

STOP RUSHING.

BE MORE PRODUCTIVE.

TIME IS NOT MONEY.
TIME IS YOUR LIFE.

Mathematics is an indispensable tool for life. From the systems that underpin our newsfeeds, through to the data analysis that informs our health and financial decisions, to the algorithms that power how we search online – mathematics is at the heart of how our modern world functions.

In 20 dip-in lessons, *Understanding Numbers* explains how and why mathematics fuels your world and arms you with the knowledge to make wiser choices in all areas of your life.

Rachel Thomas and **Marianne Freiberger** are the editors of *Plus* magazine, which publishes articles from the world's top mathematicians and science writers on topics as diverse as art, medicine, cosmology and sport (plus.maths.org).

Rachel and Marianne have co-authored the popular maths books *Numericon* and *Maths Squared*, and were editors on *50: Visions of Mathematics*. Between them they have nearly 30 years of experience writing about mathematics for a general audience.

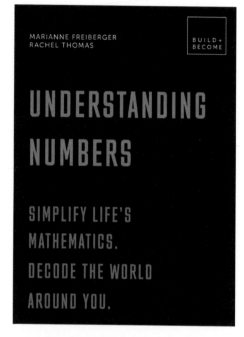

MARIANNE FREIBERGER
RACHEL THOMAS

BUILD +
BECOME

UNDERSTANDING NUMBERS

SIMPLIFY LIFE'S MATHEMATICS. DECODE THE WORLD AROUND YOU.

MATHEMATICS IS AT THE HEART OF OUR WORLD.

Whether you lead a business of thousands, are at the start of your entrepreneurial journey, or are a professional, teacher, parent or student, Conscious Leadership challenges you to be aware, awake and connected as you boldly take on your future.

In 20 proactive lessons – each including powerful practices and exercises – Neil Seligman provides you with the essential tools to increase your emotional intelligence, build stress-resilience and lead yourself and others with greater compassion, clarity and joy.

Neil Seligman is a an international mindfulness advocate, conscious visionary and author. He is the Founder of The Conscious Professional, the author of *100 Mindfulness Meditations* and the originator of Soul Portrait Photography. Neil specializes in delivering inspiring keynotes, workshops and seminars on Conscious Leadership, mindfulness and resilience to busy professionals. www.theconsciousprofessional.com.

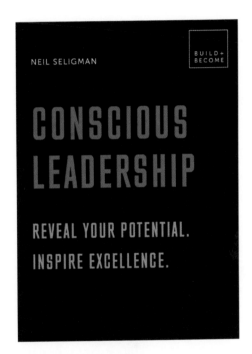

BE THE CHANGE.

Professor Elizabeth Stokoe draws on over a decade of research – from interrogations to sales enquiries, everyday talk to workplace interactions – to present 20 dip-in lessons that examine how conversations really work.

Uncover the hidden organization of the language we choose, the way we start and end conversations and the subtle, yet profound ways in which words influence us in all elements of our lives.

Talk Effectively shows how understanding how conversation works will enable you to use the tool of talk with confidence, influence and authority

Elizabeth Stokoe is Professor of Social Interaction in the Department of Social Sciences at Loughborough University, using conversation analysis to understand how talk works. Outside the University, she runs workshops with professionals using her research-based communication training method called the "Conversation Analytic Roleplay Method". She is one of thirteen WIRED 2015 Innovation Fellows; has given TEDx, *New Scientist*, SciFoo/Google, Cheltenham Science Festival and Royal Institution lectures, and her research and biography were featured on the BBC Radio 4's *The Life Scientific*.

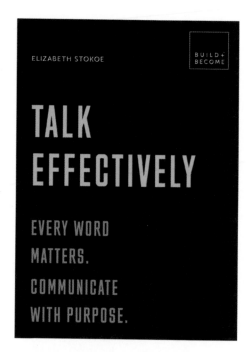

ELIZABETH STOKOE

BUILD+
BECOME

TALK EFFECTIVELY

EVERY WORD MATTERS. COMMUNICATE WITH PURPOSE.

EVERY WORD MATTERS

Using a unique, visual approach, Nathalie Spencer uncovers the science behind how we think about, use and manage money to guide you to a wiser and more enjoyable relationship with your finances.

From examining how cashless transactions affect our spending and decoding the principles of why a bargain draws you in, through to exposing what it really means to be an effective forecaster, *Good Money* reveals how you can be motivated to be better with money and provides you with essential tools to boost your financial wellbeing.

Nathalie Spencer is a behavioural scientist at Commonwealth Bank of Australia. She explores financial decision making and how insights from behavioural science can be used to boost financial wellbeing. Prior to CBA, Nathalie worked in London at ING where she wrote regularly for *eZonomics*, and at the RSA, where she co-authored *Wired for Imprudence: Behavioural Hurdles to Financial Capability*, among other titles.

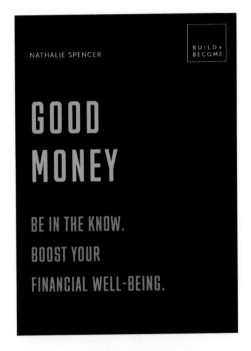

NATHALIE SPENCER

BUILD+
BECOME

GOOD MONEY

BE IN THE KNOW.
BOOST YOUR
FINANCIAL WELL-BEING.

WE ALL MAKE CHOICES WITH MONEY – UNDERSTAND YOURS.

ACKNOWLEDGEMENTS

My thanks to the Quarto team and Rachel Malig for knocking things into shape; to Stuart Tolley for the design, and to Martin Redfern at Northbank Talent Management for his guidance. Thank you to Lenneke Aalbers: first reader and a beacon of support and clarity; to Meg, Wendy, Jerry, Barbara and Jim for their wisdom, and to Michele and Kay for their suggestions. Thumbs up to Ella, Flora, Tije and Coosje.

Chris Grant is a board member, former CEO, leading keynote speaker and consultant. Chris has worked with more than 2,000 leadership and operational teams on strategy and performance, ranging from chairing one of the most successful multi-stakeholder programmes in the UK's financial and retail sectors (the Chip & PIN Programme) to helping a national sports squad prepare for a victorious European Championship campaign. Chris also chaired the board meetings of London 2012's International Inspiration Foundation.

As lead tutor on UK Sport's Elite Coach Programme – a three-year learning journey for top coaches in Olympic, Paralympic and professional sports – Chris has worked closely with some of the world's leading sports coaches. For five years, he was a member of the organizing group of the ALIA Institute in Nova Scotia, which brought together leading systems thinkers and social innovators. He continues to lead strategy and planning events in sectors ranging from medical research to property, and to pursue projects, mainly focusing on the power of sport to drive equality and justice in society.